ARE YOU FAN ENOUGH TO FACE A MOUND OF TRIVIA QUESTIONS?

You're up! But be careful. Even a baseball-trivia pinch hitter can strike out. . . .

1) Who lost more games than any other pitcher in world series play?

2) With what team did Leo Durocher break into the majors in 1928?

3) Who threw the tenth-inning home-run pitch to Rudy York in the first game of the 1946 World Series, giving the Red Sox a 3-2 victory?

4) Which of the following shortstops did not win a batting title: a)Dick Groat b)Lou Boudreau c)Luke Appling d)Luis Aparico

5) Whose line drive in the 1937 All Star Game broke Dizzy Dean's toe?

6) Who was the first infielder to wear glasses?

7) What player was nicknamed "Daddy Wags"?

Answers

1) Cleon Jones
2) The Yankees
3) Howie Pollett
4) (d) Luis Aparico
5) Earl Averill
6) George "specs" Toporcer of the 1921 Cardinals
7) Leon Wagner

SIGNET Books of Special Interest

☐ **SPORT MAGAZINE'S ALL-TIME ALL STARS edited by Tom Murray.** Profiles of 22 of baseball's greatest players by an all-star team of writers about the way each of them played the game, the way each of them lived his life, and what it takes to be the very best. (#E9169—$2.50)

☐ **THE BOYS OF SUMMER by Roger Kahn.** Roger Kahn's best-selling book of the Brooklyn Dodgers then and now recaptures "memories so keen that those of us old enough can weep, and those who are young can marvel at a world where baseball teams were the center of a love beyond the reach of intellect, and where baseball players were worshiped or hated with a fervor that made bubbles in our blood."— Heywood Hale Broun, *Chicago Tribune* (#E9288—$2.25)

☐ **SCREWBALL by Tug McGraw and Joseph Durso.** "You gotta believe!" when baseball's star reliever and super flake rips the cover off the game he plays and life he's led . . . "It's the best!"—Roger Kahn, author of *The Boys of Summer* in *The New York Times* Includes an action-packed photo insert. (#Y6421—$1.25)

☐ **THE OFFICIAL PETE ROSE SCRAPBOOK: The Life, Times and Streak of Charlie Hustle by Pete Rose.** Introduction by Hal McCoy. In his own words—the explosive story of one of baseball's most exciting players. Includes scorecards, Pete's milestones, game statistics, and more than 125 photos with his own candid captions. (#XE2054—$4.95)

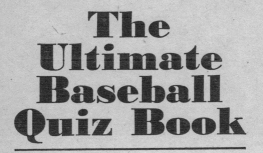

The Ultimate Baseball Quiz Book

by
Dom Forker

A SIGNET BOOK
NEW AMERICAN LIBRARY
TIMES MIRROR

PUBLISHED BY
THE NEW AMERICAN LIBRARY
OF CANADA LIMITED

To my lifetime heroes:
Ellen Gallagher Forker, my mother,
and Columb Forker, my father

NAL BOOKS ARE AVAILABLE AT QUANTITY DISCOUNTS
WHEN USED TO PROMOTE PRODUCTS OR SERVICES. FOR
INFORMATION PLEASE WRITE TO PREMIUM MARKETING
DIVISION, THE NEW AMERICAN LIBRARY, INC., 1633
BROADWAY, NEW YORK, NEW YORK 10019.

Copyright © 1981 by Dom Forker

First Printing, March, 1981

2 3 4 5 6 7 8 9

SIGNET TRADEMARK REG. U.S. PAT. OFF. AND FOREIGN COUNTRIES
REGISTERED TRADEMARK – MARCA REGISTRADA
HECHO EN WINNIPEG, CANADA

SIGNET, SIGNET CLASSICS, MENTOR, PLUME, MERIDIAN
and NAL BOOKS are published in Canada by The New American
Library of Canada, Limited, Scarborough, Ontario

PRINTED IN CANADA
COVER PRINTED IN U.S.A.

CONTENTS

Introduction

Thirty-five summers have rolled by since that sudden spring when Jackie Robinson broke the color barrier of "organized" baseball; but I still fondly remember, as though it were yesterday, that unusually warm April afternoon of 1946 when he first crossed the foul line of a "white" diamond.

At the time I was an avid fan of Frank Hague, the larcenous mayor of Jersey City, and a bitter foe of Jackie Robinson, the felonious base thief of the Montreal Royals.

Looking back to that eventful day, however, I find it easy to justify the prejudices of my nine-year-old self.

First Mayor Hague had indirectly provided me with the ticket that gained me access to Roosevelt Stadium, which was filled with 26,000 pennant-waving fans on that historic occasion.

Little did I know, at the time, that Mayor Hague expected every city employee in Jersey City to buy a quota of tickets for the opening-day game every year in order to insure a sellout. He sold so many tickets, it seemed, that he could have turned people away from the Los Angeles Coliseum.

Fortunately, for the grade-school baseball fans in the Jersey City–Bayonne area, not all of the people who bought tickets for the opener wished to attend it. Better still, many of them felt that they were getting at least part of their money's worth if they could give them away to appreciative young boys who would put them to their proper use. I was just one of many grateful youths who

1

received free tickets for the 1946 opening-day game. We proudly presented our prized possessions to the good Sisters of St. Joseph's, and we promptly got excused from all afternoon classes on that special day.

Second, I was an ardent fan of the Jersey City Giants, the Triple-A International League farm team of the parent New York Giants.

Manager Mel Ott's players were, of course, the bitter rivals of the Brooklyn Dodgers, who just happened to be the parent organization of the Montreal Royals. If you rooted for the Big Giants, you rooted for the Little Giants; if you cheered for the Dodgers, you cheered for the Royals. The rivalry was as simple as that.

So, when Jackie Robinson stepped into the batter's box in the first inning, I cheered the Jersey City Giants' pitcher and booed the Montreal Royals' second baseman. But Robinson, leaning forward like a cobra with his bat held straight up and down, seemed eager to give me a reception of his own.

And he did!

He led the Royals to a 14–1 victory with four hits, including a home run, two stolen bases, and four runs scored. By the time the game had ended, there seemed to be a lot of converts and very few Giants' fans left in the sparsely populated park.

That's the way it was back then, and in the 1950s, when we were growing up on the streets of Bayonne. From morning to night, we would form baseball comparisons that would inevitably lead to disputed deadlocks. Who's the best center fielder in New York: Joe DiMaggio, Willie Mays, or Duke Snider? Wow! Who's the best team in New York: the Yankees, the Dodgers, or the Giants? Dynamite! Who's the best manager in New York: Casey Stengel, Leo Durocher, or Charlie Dressen? Division!

I've never grown tired of talking about baseball: arguing the indefensible, conjuring up the possible, and predicting the might-have-beens. Facts, patterns, and ironic twists have always been especially appealing to me. Somehow none of it seems trivial. Anything that is connected with baseball is just too important to me.

Maybe you feel the same way! If you do, maybe you can help me. Who was that Jersey City Giants' pitcher whom I wanted to strike out Jackie Robinson, when I was young?

Dom Forker
July 28, 1980

Answer: Warren Sandell, who according to *The New York Times* "had a propensity to throw home-run pitches," never made it to the major leagues.

Chapter One

THE HITTERS

1. HOW GOOD IS .300?

Twenty of the following forty players have won at least one batting title, though they have lifetime averages of less than .300; the other twenty players have lifetime averages of .300 or better, though they have never won a batting title. Put the batting champs in the left-hand column and the .300 hitters in the right-hand column.

Mickey Mantle	Lou Boudreau
Johnny Pesky	Mickey Vernon
Enos Slaughter	Debs Garms
Tommy Davis	Sam Rice
Norm Cash	Heinie Zimmerman
Joe Cronin	Dale Mitchell
Hal Chase	Pete Reiser
George Stirnweiss	Larry Doyle
Carl Yastrzemski	Hank Greenberg
Mel Ott	Ferris Fain
Bill Dickey	Alex Johnson
Pete Runnels	Eddie Collins
Bobby Avila	Phil Cavarretta
Lloyd Waner	Earle Combs
Harry Walker	Carl Furillo
Bob Meusel	Babe Herman
Joe Jackson	Kiki Cuyler
Hack Wilson	Frankie Frisch
Earl Averill	Pie Traynor
Dick Groat	Mickey Cochrane

1) ————	1) ————
2) ————	2) ————
3) ————	3) ————
4) ————	4) ————
5) ————	5) ————
6) ————	6) ————
7) ————	7) ————
8) ————	8) ————
9) ————	9) ————
10) ————	10) ————
11) ————	11) ————
12) ————	12) ————
13) ————	13) ————
14) ————	14) ————
15) ————	15) ————
16) ————	16) ————
17) ————	17) ————
18) ————	18) ————
19) ————	19) ————
20) ————	20) ————

2. WHO DID IT TWICE?

I. National League

Five of the following ten players have won one National League batting title; the other five have won two. List the one-time winners in the left-hand column and the two-time winners in the right-hand column: Willie Mays, Lefty O'Doul, Tommy Davis, Harry Walker, Dixie Walker, Henry Aaron, Carl Furillo, Jackie Robinson, Ernie Lombardi, and Richie Ashburn.

1) _____   1) _____
2) _____   2) _____
3) _____   3) _____
4) _____   4) _____
5) _____   5) _____

II. American League

Five of the following ten players have won one American League batting title; the other five have won two. List the one-time winners in the left-hand column and the two-time winners in the right-hand column: George Kell, Al Kaline, Jimmie Foxx, Norm Cash, Luke Appling, Mickey Vernon, Mickey Mantle, Pete Runnels, Ferris Fain, and Harvey Kuenn.

1) _____   1) _____
2) _____   2) _____
3) _____   3) _____
4) _____   4) _____
5) _____   5) _____

3. THE FABULOUS FIFTIES

Ten players have hit a total of 50 or more home runs in one season: Willie Mays, Mickey Mantle, Hank Greenberg, George Foster, Jimmie Foxx, Roger Maris, Johnny Mize, Ralph Kiner, Hack Wilson, and Babe Ruth. The ten of them have done it a total of 17 times. One of them accomplished the feat four times. Four of them achieved it twice. Place them in the order of their single-season rank. Totals, years, and leagues are given as clues.

1) _____ (61) 1961 (AL)
2) _____ (60) 1927 (AL)
3) _____ (59) 1921 (AL)
4) _____ (58) 1932 (AL)
5) _____ (58) 1938 (AL)
6) _____ (56) 1930 (NL)
7) _____ (54) 1920 (AL)
8) _____ (54) 1928 (AL)
9) _____ (54) 1949 (NL)
10) _____ (54) 1961 (AL)
11) _____ (52) 1956 (AL)
12) _____ (52) 1965 (NL)
13) _____ (52) 1977 (NL)
14) _____ (51) 1947 (NL)
15) _____ (51) 1947 (NL)
16) _____ (51) 1955 (NL)
17) _____ (50) 1938 (AL)

4. THE (500) HOME RUN CLUB

There have been 12 players who have hit more than 500 home runs in their lifetimes. See how many of them you can name. Their respective totals are listed in parentheses.

1) _____ (755)
2) _____ (714)
3) _____ (660)
4) _____ (586)
5) _____ (573)
6) _____ (536)
7) _____ (534)
8) _____ (521)
9) _____ (521)
10) _____ (512)
11) _____ (512)
12) _____ (511)

5. THEY HIT FOR POWER AND AVERAGE

I. National League

Five National League players have won both the home-run crown and the batting title in the same year. One of them did it twice. Match the following players with the year(s) in which they performed the feat: Joe Medwick, Johnny Mize, Heinie Zimmerman, Rogers Hornsby (2), and Chuck Klein.

1) _____ (1912)
2) _____ (1922)
3) _____ (1925)
4) _____ (1933)
5) _____ (1937)
6) _____ (1939)

II. American League

Do the same with the following nine American Leaguers: Ted Williams (3), Lou Gehrig, Nap Lajoie, Mickey Mantle, Babe Ruth, Ty Cobb, Jimmie Foxx, Carl Yastrzemski, and Frank Robinson.

1) _____ (1901)
2) _____ (1909)
3) _____ (1924)
4) _____ (1933)
5) _____ (1934)
6) _____ (1941)
7) _____ (1942)
8) _____ (1947)
9) _____ (1956)
10) _____ (1966)
11) _____ (1967)

6. THE 3000-HIT CLUB

The following 15 players have accumulated 3000-or-more major league hits: Al Kaline, Tris Speaker, Carl Yastrzemski, Ty Cobb, Honus Wagner, Roberto Clemente, Eddie Collins, Stan Musial, Hank Aaron, Nap Lajoie, Pete Rose, Paul Waner, Cap Anson, Lou Brock, and Willie Mays. Their respective totals are included. Place the players in their proper order.

1) _____ (4192)
2) _____ (3771)
3) _____ (3630)
4) _____ (3552)
5) _____ (3515)
6) _____ (3430)
7) _____ (3311)
8) _____ (3283)
9) _____ (3251)
10) _____ (3152)
11) _____ (3109)
12) _____ (3023)
13) _____ (3022)
14) _____ (3007)
15) _____ (3000)

7. TRIPLE CROWN WINNERS

Eleven players have won the Triple Crown a total of 13 times: Carl Yastrzemski, Ted Williams (2), Rogers Hornsby (2), Mickey Mantle, Ty Cobb, Frank Robinson, Jimmie Foxx, Joe Medwick, Lou Gehrig, Chuck Klein, and Nap Lajoie. Fit them into the respective years in which they won the select award.

1) _____ (1901)
2) _____ (1909)
3) _____ (1922)
4) _____ (1925)
5) _____ (1933)
6) _____ (1933)
7) _____ (1934)
8) _____ (1937)
9) _____ (1942)
10) _____ (1947)
11) _____ (1956)
12) _____ (1966)
13) _____ (1967)

8. HIGHEST LIFETIME AVERAGE FOR POSITION

Identify the player, from the three listed at each position, who has hit for the highest lifetime average. At one position two players are tied for the lead.

I. National League

1B) _____ (.341) Bill Terry, Johnny Mize, or Stan Musial

2B) _____ (.358) Frankie Frisch, Jackie Robinson, or Rogers Hornsby

SS) _____ (.329) Arky Vaughan, Honus Wagner, or Travis Jackson

3B) _____ (.320) Joe Torre, Heinie Zimmerman, or Pie Traynor

OF) _____ (.336) Chuck Klein, Harry Walker, or Riggs Stephenson

OF) _____ (.333) Paul Waner, Babe Herman, or Zack Wheat

OF) _____ (.349) Kiki Cuyler, Stan Musial, or Lefty O'Doul

C) _____ (.306) Ernie Lombardi, Gabby Hartnett, or Roy Campanella

II. American League

1B) _____ (.340) Lou Gehrig, Jimmie Foxx, or George Sisler

2B) _____ (.339) Nap Lajoie, Charlie Gehringer, or Eddie Collins

SS) _____ (.314) Joe Cronin, Cecil Travis, or Luke Appling

3B) _____ (.307) George Kell, Frank Baker, or Jimmy Collins

OF) _____ (.367) Harry Heilmann, Tris Speaker, or Ty Cobb

OF) _____ (.356) Babe Ruth, Al Simmons, or Joe Jackson

OF) _____ (.344) Joe DiMaggio, Ted Williams, or Heinie Manush

C) _____ (.320) Mickey Cochrane, Yogi Berra, or Bill Dickey

9. HIGHEST SINGLE SEASON AVERAGE FOR POSITION

Identify the player, from the three listed at each position, who has hit for the highest average in a single season.

I. National League

1B) _____ (.401) Bill Terry, Johnny Mize, or Stan Musial

2B) _____ (.424) Frankie Frisch, Jackie Robinson, or Rogers Hornsby

SS) _____ (.385) Arky Vaughan, Honus Wagner, or Travis Jackson

3B) _____ (.372) Joe Torre, Heinie Zimmerman, or Pie Traynor

OF) _____ (.398) Paul Waner, Fred Lindstrom, or Lefty O'Doul

OF) _____ (.393) Stan Musial, Babe Herman, or Roberto Clemente

OF) _____ (.386) Chuck Klein, Zack Wheat, or Harry Walker

C) _____ (.353) Ernie Lombardi, Gabby Hartnett, or Eugene Hargrave

II. American League

1B) _____ (.420) Lou Gehrig, Jimmie Foxx, or George Sisler

2B) _____ (.422) Nap Lajoie, Charlie Gehringer, or Eddie Collins

SS) _____ (.388) Joe Cronin, Cecil Travis, or Luke Appling

3B) _____ (.347) George Kell, Frank Baker, or Jimmy Collins

OF) _____ (.420) Harry Heilmann, Tris Speaker, or Ty Cobb

OF) _____ (.408) Babe Ruth, Al Simmons, or Joe Jackson

OF) _____ (.406) Sam Crawford, Ted Williams, or Heinie Manush

C) _____ (.362) Mickey Cochrane, Yogi Berra, or Bill Dickey

10. THE YEAR THEY HIT THE HEIGHTS

Take the following ten hitters and match them up with their highest respective season's batting average: Babe Ruth, Jackie Robinson, Stan Musial, Rogers Hornsby, Charlie Keller, Ted Williams, Roberto Clemente, Ty Cobb, Joe DiMaggio, and Mickey Mantle.

1)	_____ (.424)	6)	_____ (.376)
2)	_____ (.420)	7)	_____ (.365)
3)	_____ (.406)	8)	_____ (.357)
4)	_____ (.393)	9)	_____ (.342)
5)	_____ (.381)	10)	_____ (.334)

11. MATCHING AVERAGES

Match the following ten players with their corresponding lifetime averages listed below: Rogers Hornsby, Babe Ruth, Honus Wagner, Ty Cobb, Stan Musial, Jimmy Foxx, Tris Speaker, Mickey Cochrane, Mel Ott, and Bill Terry.

1)	_____ (.367)	6)	_____ (.331)
2)	_____ (.358)	7)	_____ (.329)
3)	_____ (.344)	8)	_____ (.325)
4)	_____ (.342)	9)	_____ (.320)
5)	_____ (.341)	10)	_____ (.304)

12. ONCE IS NOT ENOUGH

Seven of the following sluggers have hit four home runs in a major league game: Babe Ruth, Lou Gehrig, Rocky Colavito, Hank Aaron, Gil Hodges, Pat Seerey, Mickey Mantle, Jimmie Foxx, Joe Adcock, Mike Schmidt, Willie Mays, Joe DiMaggio, and Hank Greenberg. Who are they?

1) _____
2) _____
3) _____
4) _____
5) _____
6) _____
7) _____

13. NATIONAL LEAGUE HOME RUN KINGS

Match the following National League home run sluggers with the number of times they have won the four-base crown: Ted Kluszewski, Johnny Mize, Ralph Kiner, Duke Snider, Eddie Mathews, Johnny Bench, Mike Schmidt, and Mel Ott.

1) _____ (7)
2) _____ (6)
3) _____ (4)
4) _____ (4)
5) _____ (2)
6) _____ (2)
7) _____ (1)
8) _____ (1)

14. WOULD YOU PINCH-HIT?

Fifteen of the best pinch-hitters in the history of the game are listed with their averages as substitute batters. Were their lifetime averages higher (Yes-No) than their pinch-hitting marks?

1) Frenchy Bordagaray (.312) _____
2) Frankie Baumholtz (.307) _____
3) Red Schoendienst (.303) _____
4) Dave Philley (.299) _____
5) Smoky Burgess (.286) _____
6) Johnny Mize (.283) _____
7) Don Mueller (.280) _____
8) Bob Johnson (.280) _____
9) Mickey Vernon (.279) _____
10) Gene Woodling (.278) _____
11) Bobby Adams (.277) _____
12) Sam Leslie (.273) _____
13) Debs Garms (.273) _____
14) Russ Nixon (.271) _____
15) Peanuts Lowrey (.270) _____

15. DECADES OF BATTING CHAMPS

Listed in the left-hand column is one batting champ from each decade and the year in which he led the league. All you have to provide is the team for which he did it.

I. National League

1) Honus Wagner (1908) _____
2) Edd Roush (1917) _____
3) Lefty O'Doul (1929) _____
4) Ernie Lombardi (1938) _____
5) Phil Cavarretta (1945) _____
6) Carl Furillo (1953) _____
7) Pete Rose (1968) _____
8) Rico Carty (1970) _____

II. American League

1) Ed Delahanty (1902) _____
2) Tris Speaker (1916) _____
3) Harry Heilmann (1923) _____
4) Luke Appling (1936) _____
5) George Stirnweiss (1945) _____
6) Ferris Fain (1951) _____
7) Pete Runnels (1962) _____
8) Alex Johnson (1970) _____

16. SUB-.320 BATTING LEADERS

Name the five players from the following ten who have won batting titles with averages that were less than .320: George Stirnweiss, Tony Oliva, Roberto Clemente, Rod Carew, Carl Yastrzemski, Ted Williams, Pete Runnels, Frank Robinson, Alex Johnson, and Elmer Flick.

1) _____ (.318) 1972
2) _____ (.316) 1966
3) _____ (.309) 1945
4) _____ (.306) 1905
5) _____ (.301) 1968

17. .390-PLUS RUNNERSUP

Name the five players from the following ten who have failed to win batting titles with averages that were better than .390: Harry Heilmann, George Sisler, Babe Ruth, Joe Jackson, Ted Williams, Rogers Hornsby, Al Simmons, Ty Cobb, Babe Herman, and Bill Terry.

1) _____ (.408) 1911
2) _____ (.401) 1922
3) _____ (.393) 1923
4) _____ (.393) 1930
5) _____ (.392) 1927

18. STEPPING INTO THE BOX

In front of the thirty players who are listed, mark an "L" (left-handed), "R" (right-handed), or "S" (switch-hitter) for the way in which they (do) hit.

1) _____ Mel Ott
2) _____ Ernie Lombardi
3) _____ Tom Tresh
4) _____ Tony Lazzeri
5) _____ Pete Rose
6) _____ Willard Marshall
7) _____ Jim Gilliam
8) _____ Wally Westlake
9) _____ Jim Gentile
10) _____ Bud Harrelson
11) _____ Granny Hamner
12) _____ Tommy Holmes
13) _____ George McQuinn
14) _____ Hector Lopez
15) _____ Smoky Burgess
16) _____ Wes Covington
17) _____ Phil Masi
18) _____ Sid Gordon
19) _____ Willie Miranda
20) _____ Maury Wills
21) _____ Nellie Fox
22) _____ Jimmie Foxx
23) _____ Red Schoendienst
24) _____ Eddie Waitkus
25) _____ Sam Mele
26) _____ Frankie Frisch
27) _____ Gino Cimoli
28) _____ Jim Rivera
29) _____ Mickey Mantle
30) _____ Roy White

Answers

1. How Good Is .300?

1) Mickey Mantle (.298)
2) Tommy Davis (.294)
3) Norm Cash (.271)
4) Hal Chase (.291)
5) George Stirnweiss (.268)
6) Carl Yastrzemski (.288)
7) Pete Runnels (.291)
8) Bobby Avila (.281)
9) Harry Walker (.296)
10) Dick Groat (.286)
11) Lou Boudreau (.295)
12) Mickey Vernon (.286)
13) Debs Garms (.293)
14) Heinie Zimmerman (.295)
15) Pete Reiser (.295)
16) Larry Doyle (.290)
17) Ferris Fain (.290)
18) Alex Johnson (.288)
19) Phil Cavarretta (.293)
20) Carl Furillo (.299)

1) Johnny Pesky (.307)
2) Enos Slaughter (.300)
3) Joe Cronin (.302)
4) Mel Ott (.304)
5) Bill Dickey (.313)
6) Lloyd Waner (.316)
7) Bob Meusel (.309)
8) Joe Jackson (.356)
9) Hack Wilson (.307)
10) Earl Averill (.318)
11) Sam Rice (.322)
12) Dale Mitchell (.312)
13) Hank Greenberg (.313)
14) Eddie Collins (.333)
15) Earle Combs (.325)
16) Babe Herman (.324)
17) Kiki Cuyler (.321)
18) Frankie Frisch (.316)
19) Pie Traynor (.320)
20) Mickey Cochrane (.320)

2. Who Did It Twice?

I. National League

1) Willie Mays
2) Harry Walker
3) Dixie Walker
4) Carl Furillo
5) Jackie Robinson

1) Lefty O'Doul
2) Tommy Davis
3) Henry Aaron
4) Ernie Lombardi
5) Richie Ashburn

II. American League

1) George Kell
2) Al Kaline
3) Norm Cash
4) Mickey Mantle
5) Harvey Kuenn

1) Jimmie Foxx
2) Luke Appling
3) Mickey Vernon
4) Pete Runnels
5) Ferris Fain

3. The Fabulous Fifties

1) Roger Maris
2) Babe Ruth
3) Babe Ruth
4) Jimmie Foxx
5) Hank Greenberg
6) Hack Wilson
7) Babe Ruth
8) Babe Ruth
9) Ralph Kiner
10) Mickey Mantle

11) Mickey Mantle
12) Willie Mays
13) George Foster
14–15) Both answers can be any combination of Johnny Mize and / or Ralph Kiner
16) Willie Mays
17) Jimmie Foxx

4. The (500) Home Run Club

1) Hank Aaron
2) Babe Ruth
3) Willie Mays
4) Frank Robinson
5) Harmon Killebrew
6) Mickey Mantle

7) Jimmie Foxx
8) Both 8–9 can be any
9) combination of Ted Williams and / or Willie McCovey

10) Both 10–11 can be
11) any combination of
    Eddie Mathews and/

or Ernie Banks
12) Mel Ott

5. They Hit For Power and Average

I. National League

1) Heinie Zimmerman
2) Rogers Hornsby
3) Rogers Hornsby
4) Chuck Klein
5) Joe Medwick
6) Johnny Mize

II. American League

1) Nap Lajoie
2) Ty Cobb
3) Babe Ruth
4) Jimmie Foxx
5) Lou Gehrig
6) Ted Williams
7) Ted Williams
8) Ted Williams
9) Mickey Mantle
10) Frank Robinson
11) Carl Yastrzemski

6. The 3000-Hit Club

1) Ty Cobb
2) Hank Aaron
3) Stan Musial
4) Pete Rose
5) Tris Speaker
6) Honus Wagner
7) Eddie Collins
8) Willie Mays

9) Nap Lajoie
10) Paul Waner
11) Carl Yastrzemski
12) Lou Brock
13) Cap Anson
14) Al Kaline
15) Roberto Clemente

7. Triple Crown Winners

1) Nap Lajoie	7) Lou Gehrig
2) Ty Cobb	8) Joe Medwick
3) Rogers Hornsby	9) Ted Williams
4) Rogers Hornsby	10) Ted Williams
5) Chuck Klein or Jimmie Foxx	11) Mickey Mantle
	12) Frank Robinson
6) Chuck Klein or Jimmie Foxx	13) Carl Yastrzemski

8. Highest Lifetime Average

I. National League	*II. American League*
1) Bill Terry	1) Lou Gehrig and George Sisler
2) Rogers Hornsby	
3) Honus Wagner	2) Nap Lajoie
4) Pie Traynor	3) Cecil Travis
5) Riggs Stephenson	4) Frank Baker
6) Paul Waner	5) Ty Cobb
7) Lefty O'Doul	6) Joe Jackson
8) Ernie Lombardi	7) Ted Williams
	8) Mickey Cochrane

9. Highest Single Season Average for Position

I. National League	*II. American League*
1) Bill Terry	1) George Sisler
2) Rogers Hornsby	2) Nap Lajoie
3) Arky Vaughan	3) Luke Appling
4) Heinie Zimmerman	4) Frank Baker
5) Lefty O'Doul	5) Ty Cobb
6) Babe Herman	6) Joe Jackson
7) Chuck Klein	7) Ted Williams
8) Eugene Hargrave	8) Bill Dickey

10. The Year They Hit The Heights

1) Rogers Hornsby
2) Ty Cobb
3) Ted Williams
4) Babe Ruth
5) Joe DiMaggio

6) Stan Musial
7) Mickey Mantle
8) Roberto Clemente
9) Jackie Robinson
10) Charlie Keller

11. Matching Averages

1) Ty Cobb
2) Rogers Hornsby
3) Tris Speaker
4) Babe Ruth
5) Bill Terry

6) Stan Musial
7) Honus Wagner
8) Jimmie Foxx
9) Mickey Cochrane
10) Mel Ott

12. Once Is Not Enough

1) Lou Gehrig
2) Rocky Colavito
3) Gil Hodges
4) Pat Seerey

5) Joe Adcock
6) Mike Schmidt
7) Willie Mays

13. National League Home Run Kings

1) Ralph Kiner
2) Mel Ott
3) Johnny Mize or
   Mike Schmidt
4) Johnny Mize or
   Mike Schmidt
5) Eddie Mathews or
   Johnny Bench

6) Eddie Mathews or
   Johnny Bench
7) Ted Kluszewski or
   Duke Snider
8) Ted Kluszewski or
   Duke Snider

14. Would You Pinch-Hit?

1) No (.283)
2) No (.290)
3) No (.289)
4) No (.270)
5) Yes (.295)
6) Yes (.312)
7) Yes (.296)
8) No (.272)
9) Yes (.286)
10) Yes (.284)
11) No (.269)
12) Yes (.304)
13) Yes (.293)
14) No (.268)
15) Yes (.273)

15. Decades of Batting Champs

I. National League

1) Pirates
2) Reds
3) Phillies
4) Reds
5) Cubs
6) Dodgers
7) Reds
8) Braves

II. American League

1) Senators
2) Indians
3) Tigers
4) White Sox
5) Yankees
6) Athletics
7) Red Sox
8) Angels

16. Sub-.320 Batting Leaders

1) Rod Carew
2) Frank Robinson
3) George Stirnweiss
4) Elmer Flick
5) Carl Yastrzemski

17. .390-Plus Runnersup

1) Joe Jackson
2) Ty Cobb
3) Babe Ruth
4) Babe Herman
5) Al Simmons

18. Stepping Into the Box

1) L	16) L
2) R	17) R
3) S	18) R
4) R	19) S
5) S	20) S
6) L	21) L
7) S	22) R
8) R	23) S
9) L	24) L
10) S	25) R
11) R	26) S
12) L	27) R
13) L	28) L
14) R	29) S
15) L	30) S

Who's on First

Bobby Thomson's game-winning home run in the final playoff game of the 1951 season gave the Giants the most dramatic come-from-behind title in the history of baseball. It also provided trivia buffs with a gold mine of facts and questions.

Sal Maglie started the game for the Giants; Don Newcombe toed the mound for the Dodgers. They hooked up in a classic pitching duel until the eighth inning when the visiting Dodgers scored three runs to take a 4–1 lead. With Maglie departed from the scene and Newcombe mowing down the Giants in the bottom of the eighth, the Dodgers seemed virtually assured of winning their sixth National League pennant. But the Giants, who had fought back from a 13½ game deficit during the regular season, were not about to give up.

Al Dark led off the bottom of the ninth by singling to center. Charlie Dressen, the manager of the Dodgers, made a tactical mistake when he did not tell first baseman Gil Hodges to play behind the runner; for Don Mueller ripped a single to right, sending Dark to third. If Hodges had been playing deep, Mueller would have hit into a double play; and the Dodgers would have cinched the pennant, for Monte Irvin, the following batter, popped out. Whitey Lockman then ripped a double, scoring Dark and sending Mueller to third. Sliding into the base, Mueller broke his ankle and was replaced by pinch runner Clint Hartung. That brought Thomson up to the plate with a free base at first. Had Dressen chosen to put the potential winning run on base, the Giants would have had to send a rookie up to the plate—Willie Mays.

Instead Dressen decided to change pitchers. He had Carl Erskine and Ralph Branca warming up in the bull pen. Erskine had looked the sharper of the two; but just before bull pen coach Clyde Sukeforth made his recommendation to Dressen, Erskine bounced a curve. That settled the matter: Branca got the call. When Branca walked in from the bull pen, some of the superstitious "faithful" from Flatbush must have got an ominous feeling when they noted the number "13" on the back of the pitcher's uniform. Coincidentally, Branca had 13 wins at the time. He also had 12 losses. After his second pitch to Thomson, which "The Staten Island Scot" hit for the pennant-winning homer, the 13's were balanced, all the way across.

Almost all of baseball's avid followers of the sport know that Branca was the losing pitcher in that fateful game. But I've run across very few baseball aficionados who know who the winning pitcher was. Do you?

Answer: Larry Jansen

Chapter Two

THE PITCHERS

19. FAMOUS HOME RUN PITCHES

Match the following pitchers with the batters to whom they threw historic home run pitches: Don Newcombe, Bob Purkey, Bob Lemon, Ralph Terry, Howie Pollet, Robin Roberts, Ralph Branca, Jack Billingham, Al Downing, and Barney Schultz.

1) _____ He threw the home run pitch to Bill Mazeroski that gave the Pirates the 1960 world series. The circuit clout gave Pittsburgh a 10–9 win.

2) _____ He threw the game-winning home run pitch to Joe DiMaggio in the top of the tenth inning in the second game of the 1950 world series. The Yankees won, 2–1.

3) _____ He threw the home run pitch to Bobby Thomson in the final playoff game of the National League's 1951 season. The Giants outlasted the Dodgers, 5–4.

4) _____ He threw the three-run homer to Dick Sisler in the top of the tenth inning of the final game of the 1950 season. The home run gave Robin Roberts the margin of victory, and it gave the Phillies the National League pennant.

5) _____ He threw the pitch that Hank Aaron hit for home run number 714.

6) _____ He threw the pitch that Hank Aaron hit for home run number 715.

7) _____ He threw the tenth-inning home run pitch to Rudy York in the first game of the 1946 world series. It gave the Red Sox a 3–2 victory.

8) _____ He threw the ninth-inning home run pitch to Mickey Mantle in the third game of the 1964 world series. It gave the Yankees a 2–1 victory.

9) _____ He threw the three-run homer to Dusty Rhodes in the bottom of the tenth inning in Game One of the 1954 world series. The blow gave the Giants a 5–2 victory.

10) _____ He threw the ninth-inning home run pitch to Roger Maris in the third game of the 1961 world series. The home run gave the Yankees a 3–2 win.

20. THE PITCHING MASTERS

Walter Johnson, Eddie Plank, Early Wynn, Cy Young, Lefty Grove, Warren Spahn, Christy Mathewson, and Grover Alexander all won 300 or more games. Put them in their proper order.

1) _____ (511)   5) _____ (363)
2) _____ (416)   6) _____ (325)
3) _____ (374)   7) _____ (300)
4) _____ (373)   8) _____ (300)

21. THE PERFECT GAME

Eight of the following 15 pitchers have thrown perfect games: Walter Johnson, Carl Hubbell, Ernie Shore, Babe Ruth, Jim Hunter, Whitey Ford, Jim Bunning, Cy Young, Robin Roberts, Bob Feller, Addie Joss, Sandy Koufax, Wes Ferrell, Don Larsen, and Charlie Robertson. Name them.

1) _____   5) _____
2) _____   6) _____
3) _____   7) _____
4) _____   8) _____

22. MULTIPLE NO-HITTERS

All of the 25 pitchers who are listed below have hurled no-hit games. Fifteen of them have done it more than once. In fact, two of them have done it four times; two of them three times; and 11 of them twice. Match the pitcher with the number that denotes how many times he performed the feat.

Bobo Holloman	Warren Spahn
Mel Parnell	Sam Jones
Johnny Vander Meer	Milt Pappas
Steve Busby	Bill Singer
Rick Wise	Carl Erskine
Ken Holtzman	Sal Maglie
Don Wilson	Bob Feller
Gaylord Perry	Virgil Trucks
Dean Chance	Allie Reynolds
Sandy Koufax	Jim Maloney
Jim Bunning	Don Larsen
Juan Marichal	Nolan Ryan
Bo Belinsky	

1) _____ (4)		9) _____ (2)	
2) _____ (4)		10) _____ (2)	
3) _____ (3)		11) _____ (2)	
4) _____ (3)		12) _____ (2)	
5) _____ (2)		13) _____ (2)	
6) _____ (2)		14) _____ (2)	
7) _____ (2)		15) _____ (2)	
8) _____ (2)			

23. BACK-TO-BACK 20-GAME WINNERS

Match the pitchers with the span of their careers when they recorded consecutive 20-game winning seasons.

1) _____ Tom Seaver	a)	1969–71
2) _____ Dave McNally	b)	1967–72
3) _____ Lefty Grove	c)	1910–19
4) _____ Paul Derringer	d)	1936–39
5) _____ Hal Newhouser	e)	1911–17
6) _____ Red Ruffing	f)	1968–69
7) _____ Warren Spahn	g)	1965–66
8) _____ Bob Feller	h)	1971–72
9) _____ Carl Hubbell	i)	1968–70
10) _____ Bob Lemon	j)	1963–66
11) _____ Denny McLain	k)	1933–37
12) _____ Vic Raschi	l)	1970–73
13) _____ Christy Mathewson	m)	1948–50
14) _____ Grover Cleveland Alexander	n)	1938–40
15) _____ Don Newcombe	o)	1903–14
16) _____ Juan Marichal	p)	1927–33
17) _____ Mike Cuellar	q)	1949–51
18) _____ Bob Gibson	r)	1942–44
19) _____ Walter Johnson	s)	1968–71
20) _____ Robin Roberts	t)	1939–41, 1946–47*
21) _____ Sandy Koufax	u)	1950–55
22) _____ Mort Cooper	v)	1956–61
23) _____ Ferguson Jenkins	w)	1944–46
24) _____ Jim Palmer	x)	1955–56
25) _____ Dizzy Dean	y)	1933–36

* The pitcher's consecutive string of 20-win seasons was interrupted by the war.

24. THE FLAMETHROWERS

Name the ten flamethrowers from the following **17 who** have struck out more than 300 batters in one season: Nolan Ryan, Tom Seaver, Sandy Koufax, Ferguson Jenkins, Mickey Lolich, Sam McDowell, Jim Lonborg, Bob Feller, Steve Carlton, Herb Score, Jim Bunning, Walter Johnson, Don Drysdale, Bob Gibson, Rube Waddell, Vida Blue, and J. R. Richard.

1) _____   6) _____
2) _____   7) _____
3) _____   8) _____
4) _____   9) _____
5) _____   10) _____

25. BLUE-CHIP PITCHERS

Ten of the 20 pitchers who are listed below have recorded winning percentages of .600 or better. Who are they?

Whitey Ford	Jim Perry
Ted Lyons	Vic Raschi
Early Wynn	Jim Kaat
Allie Reynolds	Don Drysdale
Jim Palmer	Sal Maglie
Robin Roberts	Dizzy Dean
Gaylord Perry	Sandy Koufax
Mort Cooper	Mickey Lolich
Tom Seaver	Claude Osteen
Waite Hoyt	Lefty Gomez

1) _____   6) _____
2) _____   7) _____
3) _____   8) _____
4) _____   9) _____
5) _____   10) _____

26. 200 TIMES A LOSER

Ten of the 20 pitchers listed below have lost 200 or more major league games. Name them.

Cy Young	Bob Feller
Billy Pierce	Red Ruffing
Christy Mathewson	Milt Pappas
Bobo Newsom	Carl Hubbell
Walter Johnson	Paul Derringer
Juan Marichal	Robin Roberts
Mel Harder	Bob Gibson
Warren Spahn	Bob Friend
Grover Alexander	Early Wynn
Lefty Grove	Jim Bunning

1) ———   6) ———
2) ———   7) ———
3) ———   8) ———
4) ———   9) ———
5) ———   10) ———

27. WINDING UP

Mark "L" in the space provided for the pitchers who threw left-handed and "R" for the hurlers who threw right-handed. There are an even number of each contained in the list.

1) _____ Hal Newhouser
2) _____ Vernon Gomez
3) _____ Mike Garcia
4) _____ Eddie Lopat
5) _____ Virgil Trucks
6) _____ Ellis Kinder
7) _____ Billy Pierce
8) _____ Herb Score
9) _____ Bucky Walters
10) _____ Van Lingle Mungo
11) _____ Vic Raschi
12) _____ Johnny Sain
13) _____ Preacher Roe
14) _____ Dave Koslo
15) _____ Billy Loes
16) _____ Ned Garver
17) _____ Billy Hoeft
18) _____ Don Mossi
19) _____ Frank Lary
20) _____ Max Lanier
21) _____ Harry Brecheen
22) _____ Johnny Podres
23) _____ Larry Jansen
24) _____ Lew Burdette
25) _____ Mudcat Grant
26) _____ Vernon Law
27) _____ Mel Parnell
28) _____ Rip Sewell
29) _____ Tommy Byrne
30) _____ Ron Perranoski

19. Famous Home Run Pitches

1) Ralph Terry
2) Robin Roberts
3) Ralph Branca
4) Don Newcombe
5) Jack Billingham
6) Al Downing
7) Howie Pollet
8) Barney Schultz
9) Bob Lemon
10) Bob Purkey

20. The Pitching Masters

1) Cy Young
2) Walter Johnson
3) Christy Mathewson
4) Grover Alexander
5) Warren Spahn
6) Eddie Plank
7) Lefty Grove or Early Wynn
8) Lefty Grove or Early Wynn

21. The Perfect Game

1) Ernie Shore
2) Jim Hunter
3) Jim Bunning
4) Cy Young
5) Addie Joss
6) Sandy Koufax
7) Don Larsen
8) Charlie Robertson

22. Multiple No-hitters

1) Nolan Ryan or Sandy Koufax
2) Nolan Ryan or Sandy Koufax
3) Bob Feller or Jim Maloney
4) Bob Feller or Jim Maloney

Johnny Vander Meer, Steve Busby, Ken Holtzman, Jim Bunning, Don Wilson, Dean Chance, Warren Spahn, Sam Jones, Carl

5–15) Any combination
      of the following:

Erskine, Virgil
Trucks, Allie
Reynolds

23. Back-to-Back 20-Game Winners

1) h		14) e
2) s		15) x
3) p		16) j
4) n		17) a
5) w		18) i
6) d		19) c
7) v		20) u
8) t		21) g
9) k		22) r
10) m		23) b
11) f		24) l
12) q		25) y
13) o		

24. The Flamethrowers

1) Nolan Ryan
2) Sandy Koufax
3) Mickey Lolich
4) Sam McDowell
5) Bob Feller
6) Steve Carlton
7) Walter Johnson
8) Rube Waddell
9) Vida Blue
10) J. R. Richard

25. Blue-Chip Pitchers

1) Whitey Ford (.690)
2) Allie Reynolds (.630)
3) Jim Palmer (.646)
4) Mort Cooper (.631)
5) Tom Seaver (.635)
6) Vic Raschi (.667)
7) Sal Maglie (.657)
8) Dizzy Dean (.644)
9) Sandy Koufax (.655)
10) Lefty Gomez (.649)

26. 200 Times a Loser

1) Cy Young
2) Bobo Newsom
3) Walter Johnson
4) Warren Spahn
5) Grover Alexander
6) Red Ruffing
7) Paul Derringer
8) Robin Roberts
9) Bob Friend
10) Early Wynn

27. Winding Up

1) L
2) L
3) R
4) L
5) R
6) R
7) L
8) L
9) R
10) R
11) R
12) R
13) L
14) L
15) R
16) R
17) L
18) L
19) R
20) L
21) L
22) L
23) R
24) R
25) R
26) R
27) L
28) R
29) L
30) L

Who's on First

The pitcher who threw the best game that has ever been spun lost the decision. If you don't believe me, you can look it up. Or, better still, you could ask Harvey Haddix.

On May 26, 1959, the Pirates' left hander pitched a perfect game for nine innings against the host Braves. That puts him in the select company of Cy Young, Addie Joss, Ernie Shore, Charlie Robertson, Don Larsen, Jim Bunning, Sandy Koufax, and Jim Hunter, the only other pitchers who have thrown a nine-inning perfect game in the modern era. But Haddix was not as fortunate as his select peers. Their teams gave them sufficient support to win the games. Haddix' club did not.

So "The Kitten" was forced to prove that he could pitch a game that had never been thrown before. He put the Braves down one, two, three in the tenth; he mowed them down in order in the eleventh; and he sailed through the lineup in sequence in the twelfth. But still his teammates, though they had touched Lew Burdette for 12 hits, could not dent the plate the one time that was needed to give their special southpaw instant immortality.

Inning 13 proved to be unlucky for Haddix. Felix Mantilla, the first batter, reached first when third baseman Don Hoak made a throwing error on an easy ground ball. Eddie Mathews bunted Mantilla into scoring position. Haddix was then forced to intentionally pass Hank Aaron to set up the double play for the slow-running Joe Adcock. But Adcock crossed up the strategy by hitting a three-run homer to right center.

Yet the final score was only 1–0. And Haddix got credit for another out. Technically, he could have been credited with an additional out. If he had, he might have gotten out of the inning without a run being scored.

Can you unravel that strange sequence of circumstances?

Answer: Hank Aaron, the runner on first base, thought that Joe Adcock's game-winning hit had remained in play; so, when he saw Felix Mantilla racing toward home, he assumed that the one run would automatically bring the game to an end. Consequently, shortly after rounding second base, he stopped and headed for the dugout. Adcock, who had not noticed Aaron's error in judgment, naturally passed his teammate. Since the hitter had illegally passed the base runner, he was ruled out by the umpire. Aaron, on the other hand, could have been called out for illegally running the base paths. If both runners had been called out before Mantilla crossed home plate, no run would count because the third out would have been recorded before the winning run scored. But Mantilla did score and the Braves did win.

And Harvey Haddix has become an asterisk!

Chapter Three

MULTIPLE CHOICE

28. FOUR BASES TO SCORE

1) Who were the Dodger runners when Cookie Lavagetto's game-winning double with two outs in the bottom of the ninth inning broke up Bill Bevens' no-hitter in the 1947 world series?
   a. Jackie Robinson and Eddie Stanky b. Eddie Miksis and Pete Reiser c. Jackie Robinson and Spider Jorgensen d. Al Gionfriddo and Eddie Miksis

2) Whom did Don Larsen strike out for the final out in his perfect game in the 1956 world series?
   a. Gil Hodges b. Roy Campanella c. Dale Mitchell d. Carl Furillo

3) Against whom did Willie Mays hit his first major league home run?
   a. Bob Buhl b. Warren Spahn c. Larry Jansen d. Robin Roberts

4) Against whom did Hank Aaron hit his first major league home run?
   a. Curt Simmons b. Vic Raschi c. Lew Burdette d. Don Newcombe

5) Who hit the last home run in the initial Yankee Stadium?
   a. Duke Sims b. Norm Cash c. Carl Yastrzemski d. Bobby Murcer?

6) Who hit the first home run in Shea Stadium?
   a. Willie Stargell b. Frank Thomas c. Stan Musial d. Frank Howard

7) Who were the Giant runners when Bobby Thomson hit the playoff home run against the Dodgers in 1951 to decide the pennant?

a. Don Mueller and Whitey Lockman b. Al Dark and Don Mueller c. Whitey Lockman and Al Dark d. Clint Hartung and Whitey Lockman

8) Which team was the last all-white club that won the American League pennant?

a. the 1947 Yankees b. the 1953 Yankees c. the 1959 White Sox d. the 1965 Twins

9) Who hit .400 in world series play a record three times?

a. Ty Cobb b. Babe Ruth c. Lou Gehrig d. Eddie Collins

10) Who was the only Yankee who has won two batting titles?

a. Joe DiMaggio b. Mickey Mantle c. Lou Gehrig d. Babe Ruth

11) Who was doubled off first when Sandy Amoros made the game-saving catch on Yogi Berra's fly ball in the seventh inning of the seventh game of the 1955 world series between the Dodgers and the Yankees?

a. Billy Martin b. Elston Howard c. Gil McDougald d. Hank Bauer

12) Which team holds the American League record of 111 wins in one season?

a. the 1946 Red Sox b. the 1927 Yankees c. the 1959 White Sox d. the 1954 Indians

13) In addition to George Brett and Fred Lynn, who has been the only non-Twin to win the American League batting title since 1969?

a. Carl Yastrzemski b. Alex Johnson c. Frank Robinson d. Bobby Murcer

14) Who was the last player in the majors—before Brett hit .390 in 1980? Who batted better than .375 in one season?

a. Ted Williams b. Roberto Clemente c. Rod
d. Stan Musial

15) Which National League team holds the major league record of 116 wins in one season?

    a. the 1906 Cubs b. the 1930 Cardinals c. the 1952 Dodgers d. the 1976 Reds

16) Which of the following players has not recorded 500 putouts in one season?

    a. Joe DiMaggio b. Dom DiMaggio c. Vince DiMaggio d. Richie Ashburn

17) Who is the only player who has won home run titles in both leagues?

    a. Frank Robinson b. Sam Crawford c. Hank Greenberg d. Johnny Mize

18) Who is the only player who has won batting titles in both leagues?

    a. Lefty O'Doul b. Dixie Walker c. Rogers Hornsby d. Ed Delahanty

19) Who was the last player who hit more than 50 home runs in one season?

    a. Mickey Mantle b. Roger Maris c. George Foster d. Willie McCovey

20) Which of these former Yankees did not play in a world series with a National League club?

    a. Roger Maris b. Bill Skowron c. Hank Borowy d. Vic Raschi

21) Which of the following players did not win the RBI title with two teams in the same league?

    a. Orlando Cepeda b. Vern Stephens c. Johnny Mize d. Ralph Kiner

22) Which of the following pitchers did not lose more games than he won?

    a. Bobo Newsom b. Murray Dickson c. Bob Friend d. Dizzy Trout

23) Whose line drive, which almost provided the margin

victory, did Bobby Richardson catch for the final out of the 1962 world series?

a. Willie McCovey b. Jim Davenport c. Jose Pagan d. Orlando Cepeda

24) Which of the following pitchers won the first playoff game in American League history?

a. Denny Galehouse b. Bob Feller c. Gene Bearden d. Mel Parnell

25) Who was the losing pitcher for the Dodgers on the day that Don Larsen threw his perfect game in the 1956 world series?

a. Clem Labine b. Johnny Podres c. Don Newcombe d. Sal Maglie

26) Which of the following umpires worked his last game behind the plate on the day that Don Larsen pitched his perfect game?

a. Jocko Conlan b. Augie Donatelli c. Babe Pinelli d. George Magerkurth

27) Which one of the following players won back-to-back American League batting titles in the 1950s?

a. Al Rosen b. Bobby Avila c. Ferris Fain d. Al Kaline

28) Which one of the following players won back-to-back National League batting titles in the 1960s?

a. Matty Alou b. Dick Groat c. Tommy Davis d. Richie Ashburn

29) Which one of the following shortstops did not win a batting title?

a. Dick Groat b. Lou Boudreau c. Luke Appling d. Luis Aparicio

30) What was the name of the midget whom Bill Veeck sent up to the plate to pinch-hit for the Browns?

a. Frank Gabler b. Ed Gallagher c. Dick Kokos d. Eddie Gaedel

31) Which one of the following first basemen was the only right-handed hitter?

a. Gordy Coleman b. Dick Gernert c. Norm Cash
d. Luke Easter

32) Which one of the following catchers never won an MVP award?

a. Yogi Berra b. Bill Dickey c. Roy Campanella
d. Johnny Bench

33) Which one of the following players did not win the MVP award three times?

a. Joe DiMaggio b. Stan Musial c. Willie Mays
d. Roy Campanella

34) Which runner stole home a record two times in world series play?

a. Bob Meusel b. Ty Cobb c. Lou Brock d. Jackie Robinson

35) Which one of the following teams did not win four world's championships in one decade?

a. the 1910 Red Sox b. the 1920 Giants c. the 1930 Yankees d. the 1940 Yankees

36) Who was the last National League batter who hit .400?

a. Rogers Hornsby b. Lefty O'Doul c. Bill Terry
d. Arky Vaughan

37) Against whom did Babe Ruth "call his shot" in the 1932 world series?

a. Lon Warneke b. Guy Bush c. Burleigh Grimes
d. Charlie Root

38) Who hit the "homer in the dark" for the Cubs in 1938?

a. Gabby Hartnett b. Billy Herman c. Stan Hack
d. Phil Cavarretta

39) Who misplayed two outfield fly balls for the Cubs when the Athletics rallied with ten runs in the seventh inning of the fourth game of the 1929 world series to win, 10–8?

a. Kiki Cuyler b. Riggs Stephenson c. Cliff Heathcote
d. Hack Wilson

40) Which one of the following teams won the most recent pennant?

a. the Browns b. the Phillies c. the Senators d. the Cubs

41) Who has been the only American League player, in addition to Ty Cobb, who twice hit over .400?

a. Joe Jackson b. Nap Lajoie c. George Sisler d. Harry Heilmann

42) Who was the last National League pitcher who won 30 games in a season?

a. Carl Hubbell b. Dizzy Dean c. Robin Roberts d. Sandy Koufax

43) Who compiled the highest career batting average for left handers in the history of the National League?

a. Lefty O'Doul b. Bill Terry c. Stan Musial d. Paul Waner

44) Who holds the National League record for playing in the most consecutive games (1,117)?

a. Gus Suhr b. Stan Musial c. Billy Williams d. Tommy Holmes

45) Whose modern-day mark did Joe DiMaggio surpass when he batted safely in 56 consecutive games?

a. George Sisler b. Heinie Manush c. Ty Cobb d. Al Simmons

46) Which one of Babe Ruth's following teammates was the only Yankee to hit more home runs in one season than the "Sultan of Swat" during the 1920s?

a. Bob Meusel b. Lou Gehrig c. Tony Lazzeri d. Bill Dickey

47) Which pitcher came the closest to duplicating Johnny Vander Meer's feat of hurling consecutive no-hitters?

a. Nolan Ryan b. Sandy Koufax c. Virgil Trucks d. Ewell Blackwell

48) Which one of the following players did not conclude his career with the Mets?

a. Richie Ashburn b. Gil Hodges c. Gene Woodling
d. Eddie Yost

49) Which one of the following catchers did not make an error in 117 games during the 1946 season?
a. Buddy Rosar b. Frank Hayes c. Del Rice
d. Mickey Owens

50) Which one of the following teams didn't Bucky Harris manage?
a. the Phillies b. the Tigers c. the Senators d. the Braves

51) Who, in addition to Babe Ruth, has been the only left-handed batter who ever finished a season *in* the '50s in home runs?
a. Roger Maris b. Johnny Mize c. Mel Ott d. Lou Gehrig

52) Who holds the American League record for shutouts in one season by a left-handed pitcher?
a. Babe Ruth and Ron Guidry b. Lefty Grove c. Whitey Ford d. Mel Parnell

53) Who was the youngest player who has ever been elected to the Hall of Fame?
a. Ted Williams b. Roberto Clemente c. Sandy Koufax d. Dizzy Dean

54) Which one of the following players did not hit two grand slams in one game?
a. Frank Robinson b. Frank Howard c. Tony Cloninger d. Jim Northrup

55) Which one of the following Yankees stole home the most times (10) in the club's history?
a. Lou Gehrig b. Ben Chapman c. Phil Rizzuto
d. George Stirnweiss

56) Who holds the American League record for stealing home the most times (7) in one season?
a. Ty Cobb b. Eddie Collins c. Rod Carew d. Bert Campaneris

57) Who holds the National League record for stealing home the most times (7) in one season?

a. Jackie Robinson b. Pete Reiser c. Lou Brock d. Maury Wills

58) Who were the three players on the same team who hit more than 40 home runs each in the same season?

a. Babe Ruth, Lou Gehrig, Bob Meusel b. Hank Aaron, Dave Johnson, Darrell Evans c. Hank Aaron, Eddie Mathews, Wes Covington d. Johnny Mize, Willard Marshall, Walker Cooper

59) Who was the first black coach in the American League?

a. Larry Doby b. Elston Howard c. Minnie Minoso d. Satchel Paige

60) Who was the first black coach in the National League?

a. Ernie Banks b. Joe Black c. Jim Gilliam d. Willie Mays

61) Who started the double play that ended Joe DiMaggio's 56-game hitting streak?

a. Ken Keltner b. Lou Boudreau c. Ray Mack d. Hal Trosky

62) What was the most money that the Yankees ever paid Babe Ruth for a season?

a. $100,000 b. $125,000 c. $75,000 d. $80,000

63) Which pair of players did not tie for a National League home run title?

a. Ralph Kiner–Johnny Mize b. Ralph Kiner–Hank Sauer c. Willie McCovey–Hank Aaron d. Willie Mays–Hank Aaron

64) Which pair of players did not tie for an American League home run title?

a. Hank Greenberg–Jimmy Foxx b. Carl Yastrzemski–Harmon Killebrew c. Babe Ruth–Lou Gehrig d. Reggie Jackson–Dick Allen

65) Who hit the first home run in the initial Yankee Stadium?

a. Babe Ruth b. Wally Pipp c. Bob Meusel d. Joe Dugan

66) Who hit the first home run in the renovated Yankee Stadium?

a. Dan Ford b. Tony Oliva c. Graig Nettles d. Chris Chambliss

67) Who led the National League in home runs for the most consecutive years (7)?

a. Chuck Klein b. Mel Ott c. Ralph Kiner d. Hank Aaron

68) Who were the two players who hit five grand slams in one season?

a. Jim Northrup–Ralph Kiner b. Willie McCovey–Frank Robinson c. Ernie Banks–Jim Gentile d. Harmon Killebrew–Eddie Mathews

69) Who has pitched the most consecutive shutouts (6) in one season?

a. Bob Gibson b. Sal Maglie c. Walter Johnson d. Don Drysdale

70) Which one of the following pitchers did not strike out 19 batters in one game?

a. Bob Feller b. Steve Carlton c. Nolan Ryan d. Tom Seaver

71) Who was the first major leaguer who hit .400 in a season?

a. Ty Cobb b. Nap Lajoie c. Joe Jackson d. George Sisler

72) Who broke Ty Cobb's run of nine straight batting titles in 1916?

a. Tris Speaker b. George Sisler c. Hal Chase d. Harry Heilmann

73) Who was the only non-Yankee who won a home run title in the 1920s?

a. Al Simmons b. Goose Goslin c. Ken Williams d. Jimmy Foxx

74) Which one of the following American Leaguers did not win back-to-back batting titles?

a. Ted Williams b. Pete Runnels c. Joe DiMaggio d. Carl Yastrzemski

75) Which one of the following National Leaguers did not win back-to-back batting titles?

a. Pete Rose b. Roberto Clemente c. Stan Musial d. Jackie Robinson

76) Which one of the following pitchers lost a ground ball "in the sun" in a world series game?

a. Lefty Gomez b. Billy Loes c. Dave Koslo d. Vida Blue

77) With what team did Red Ruffing conclude his career?

a. the Red Sox b. the Yankees c. the Athletics d. the White Sox

78) Against whom did Mickey Mantle hit his last world series home run?

a. Curt Simmons b. Barney Schultz c. Harvey Haddix d. Bob Gibson

79) Which one of the following Cub players was called "Swish"?

a. Stan Hack b. Phil Cavarretta c. Billy Jurges d. Bill Nicholson

80) Which one of the following players had a career which did not span four decades?

a. Stan Musial b. Ted Williams c. Mickey Vernon d. Early Wynn

81) Which one of the following managers did not win a pennant in both leagues?

a. Joe McCarthy b. Bill McKechnie c. Yogi Berra d. Al Dark

82) Which one of the following Red pitchers played more than 200 games at third base?

a. Paul Derringer b. Jim Maloney c. Bob Purkey d. Bucky Walters

54

83) Which pitcher who won three games in the 1912 world series later starred in the outfield for another American League team that played in the 1920 "Autumn Classic"?

a. Babe Ruth b. Joe Wood c. Duffy Lewis d. Harry Hooper

84) Which former Yankee pitcher switched to the outfield and compiled a .349 lifetime average?

a. Rube Bressler b. Dixie Walker c. Lefty O'Doul d. Babe Ruth

85) Which of the following Yankee players came up to the majors as a pitcher, switched to the outfield, and ended his big league career on the mound?

a. Johnny Lindell b. Cliff Mapes c. Marius Russo d. Ernie Bonham

86) Which pair of the following players comprised a major league battery?

a. Ted Lyons–Buddy Rosar b. Ellis Kinder–Ernie Lombardi c. Allie Reynolds–Bill Dickey d. Rex Barney–Bruce Edwards

87) Which one of the following players had the nickname of "Lucky"?

a. Whitey Lockman b. Jack Lohrke c. Jim Lemon d. Ted Lepcio

88) Who was the player who once hit three home runs in one game off Whitey Ford?

a. Clyde Vollmer b. Dick Gernert c. Pat Seerey d. Jim Lemon

89) Which one of the following one-two punches had the most home runs on the same team?

a. Babe Ruth–Lou Gehrig b. Mickey Mantle–Roger Maris c. Hank Aaron–Eddie Mathews d. Ernie Banks–Ron Santo

90) Which one of the following pitchers took a timeout in world series play to watch a plane fly overhead?

a. Daffy Dean b. Dizzy Trout c. Lefty Gomez d. Dazzy Vance

91) Which pair of the following brothers competed against each other in world series play?

    a. Dizzy and Daffy Dean b. Jim and Gaylord Perry c. Ken and Clete Boyer d. Matty and Felipe Alou

92) Which one of the following players was not a member of the "Whiz Kids"?

    a. Andy Seminick b. Russ Meyer c. Mike Goliat d. Harry Walker

93) Which one of the following pitchers was the only one to lose a world series game?

    a. Jack Coombs b. Herb Pennock c. Lefty Gomez d. Catfish Hunter

94) Who was the only Phillie pitcher before 1980 who won a world series game?

    a. Grover Cleveland Alexander b. Robin Roberts c. Eppa Rixey d. Jim Konstanty

95) Which one of the following players did not "jump" to the Mexican League?

    a. Mickey Owen b. Luis Olmo c. Johnny Hopp d. Max Lanier

96) Who made a shoestring catch of an infield fly to save a world series?

    a. Billy Herman b. Billy Johnson c. Billy Martin d. Bobby Avila

97) Which one of the Indians' "Big Four" won a world series game with another American League team?

    a. Bob Feller b. Bob Lemon c. Mike Garcia d. Early Wynn

98) Which one of the following players did not win an American League home run title with a total below 30?

    a. Babe Ruth b. Nick Etten c. Vern Stephens d. Reggie Jackson

99) Which one of the following players did not win a National League home run crown with a total below 30?

    a. Hack Wilson b. Johnny Mize c. Ralph Kiner d. Mike Schmidt

100) Which one of the following players once hit 54 home runs in a season but did not win the league's home run title?

a. Ralph Kiner b. Willie Mays c. Mickey Mantle d. Hank Greenberg

Answers

28. Four Bases to Score

1) d
2) c
3) b
4) b
5) a
6) a
7) d
8) b
9) d (1910, 1913, and 1917)
10) a (1939–40)
11) c
12) d
13) b (1970)
14) c (.388 in 1977)
15) a
16) a
17) b (1901, Reds; 1908 and 1914, Tigers)
18) d (.410 with 1899 Phillies and .376 with 1902 Senators)
19) c (52 in 1977)
20) d
21) d
22) d (170–161)
23) a
24) c (for the 1948 Indians)
25) d
26) c
27) c (1951–52)
28) c (1962–63)

29) d
30) d
31) b
32) b
33) c
34) a
35) b
36) c (.401 in 1930)
37) d
38) a
39) d
40) b (1980)
41) c (.407 in 1920 and .420 in 1922)
42) b (30–7 in 1934)
43) a (.349)
44) c
45) a (41)
46) a (33–25 in 1925)
47) d (1947) He came two outs short of duplicating the feat.
48) d
49) a
50) d
51) b (51 in 1947)
52) a (9)
53) c (36)
54) b
55) a
56) c
57) b
58) b (1973)
59) b

60) c
61) b
62) d
63) d
64) d
65) a (1923)
66) a (1976)
67) c (1946–52)
68) c
69) d (1968)
70) a
71) b (.422 in 1901)
72) a
73) c (1922)
74) b
75) d
76) b
77) d (1947)
78) d (1964)
79) d
80) a
81) b

82) d
83) b (the Indians)
84) c
85) a
86) d
87) b
88) d
89) c (1226)
90) c
91) c (1964)
92) d
93) d (Hunter was 5–3 in series play.)
94) a (1915)
95) c
96) c (1952)
97) d (1959, with the White Sox)
99) d
98) d
100) c (1961)

Who's on First

Most umpires know the rule book from cover to cover. But occasionally a situation that is not covered by the rule book takes place. Then the umpires are in trouble.

Take, for example, the uproar that Herman "Germany" Schaefer created with his zany base running in a game between the Senators and the White Sox in 1911. With the score tied and two outs in the ninth inning, the Senators put runners on the corners, Clyde Milan on third and Schaefer on first. That's the moment when Schaefer decided to create confusion.

On the first pitch to a weak batter, Schaefer promptly stole second without a throw from the catcher. On the next pitch he proceeded to steal first, once again without a throw, but this time with a storm of protest from the White Sox bench. What base was Schaefer entitled to, the Sox wanted to know. The umpires thumbed through the rule book, but they failed to find any clause that prevented a runner from stealing any base that he had previously occupied. So, on the following pitch, Schaefer did the predictable: he stole second again. The frustrated catcher finally relented and threw the ball to second base. But Schaefer beat the throw and Milan raced home with the winning run.

Shortly thereafter, an amendment to the rule book was made: no base runner could steal a base out of sequence. The rulesmakers decided that Schaefer had tried to make a travesty of the game.

Another bizarre base running feat took place in 1963. This time it involved a Met runner, Jimmy Piersall, who was coming to the end of a celebrated—and clownish—career. In the game in which he hit his 100th career homer, he did something which indelibly impressed the event in the minds of all of the people who saw it: he ran around the bases backwards.

Once again the umpires pored through the fine print of the rule book. But it was of little or no avail: there was no rule which prevented a runner from circling the bases backwards after he had hit a home run. Shortly thereafter, however, there was. The rulesmakers once again concluded that the runner (Piersall) had tried to make a mockery of the game. So today, batters who hit home runs have to touch the bases in their proper order.

One more ludicrous baseball situation took place in St. Louis in 1951. In a game between the hometown Browns and the Tigers, the always innovative owner of St. Louis, Bill Veeck, staged a scene that baseball fans still laugh about. In the first inning of the second game of a doubleheader, Zach Taylor, the manager of St. Louis, sent a midget up to the plate to pinch-hit for the leadoff batter, Frank Saucier. The umpires demanded that Taylor put an end to the farce. But Taylor was ready for them, rule book in hand: there was no provision in the baseball guide that prevented the batter with the number ⅛ on his back from taking his turn at the plate. The next day, you can feel safe to assume, there was.

But before the amendment was made, the batter walked on four consecutive pitches before giving way to a pinch-hitter. What most probably comes readily to mind is the name of the midget, Eddie Gaedel. He is the subject of an often-asked trivia question. But what might not come so quickly to mind is the name of the pitcher who threw to the smallest target in baseball history, the name of the catcher who gave the lowest target in the history of the game, and the umpire who had the smallest strike zone in the annals of the sport.

Consider yourself to be in the ranks of a select few if you can name two of the three individuals who figured prominently in one of the most bizarre pitcher-batter confrontations that has ever taken place.

Answer: Bob Cain, pitcher; Bob Swift, catcher; and Bill Stewart, umpire

Chapter Four

FROM RUTH TO REGGIE

29. FROM RUTH TO REGGIE

1) _____ Which slugger (1933–47) missed almost six years of playing time because of the Second World War and injuries and still managed to hit 331 career home runs?

2) _____ Which Indian pitcher, who was 15–0 at the time, lost his only game of the year in his last start?

3) _____ Whose line drive in the 1937 All Star Game broke Dizzy Dean's toe?

4) _____ Which White Sox pitcher lost one of his legs in a hunting accident?

5) _____ Who was the Indian manager whom the players petitioned the Cleveland owners to fire in 1940?

6) _____ Who pitched a no-hitter on the opening day of the 1940 season?

7) _____ Who was the only player to win the Rookie of the Year award, the Most Valuable Player award, and the Triple Crown?

8) _____ Whose home run on the final day of the 1945 season won the pennant for the Tigers?

9) _____ Whose home run on the final night of the 1976 season won the pennant for the Yankees?

10) _____ Which pitcher, who was acquired from the Yankees, led the Cubs to the pennant in 1945?

11) _____ Who scored the only run in the first game of the 1948 world series after Bob Feller "almost" picked him off second base?

12) _____ Who was the manager of the Red Sox in 1948–49 when they lost the pennants on the last day of the season?

13) _____ Who was the last playing manager before Frank Robinson?

14) _____ Who was the last playing manager who led his team to a pennant?

15) _____ Who was the name star that the Yankees traded to the Indians for Allie Reynolds in 1948?

16) _____ Who was the American League home run king of 1959 who was traded after the season for batting champ Harvey Kuenn?

17) _____ Which former Giant relief specialist, then with the Orioles, threw the pitch that Mickey Mantle hit for his 500th home run?

18) _____ Who invented the "Williams's Shift"?

19) _____ Which slugging American League outfielder broke his elbow in the 1950 All Star Game?

20) _____ Which Dodger outfielder did Richie Ashburn throw out at the plate in the ninth inning of the last game of the 1950 season to send the Phillies into extra innings and subsequently the world series?

21) _____ Who threw a no-hitter in his first major league start?

22) _____ Who threw the pitch that Mickey Mantle hit for his 565-foot home run?

23) _____ Which manager did Walter O'Malley fire for demanding a three-year contract?

24) _____ Who was the 20-game season winner and the two-game world series winner for the Giants in 1954 whom they acquired from the Braves for Bobby Thomson?

25) _____ Who took Bobby Thomson's center-field position for the Giants?

26) _____ Who took Bobby Thomson's left-field position—when he broke his ankle—for the Milwaukee Braves?

27) _____ Which Indian slugging outfielder–first baseman was afflicted with polio in 1955?

28) _____ Which pitcher did Joe Adcock literally run off the mound in the early 1950s?

29) _____, Dave McNally, Jim Palmer, and Mike Cuellar were 20-game winners for the Orioles in 1971.

30) _____ Who was the one-time "Wildman" for the Yankees who lost the final game of the 1955 world series to the Dodgers' Johnny Podres, 2–0?

31) _____ Which versatile infielder hit the line drive which struck Herb Score in the eye?

32) _____ Which pitcher, picked up on waivers from the Indians, won 13 games down the stretch, including a no-hitter against the Phillies, to pitch the Dodgers to the 1956 pennant?

33) _____ Who hit two two-run homers against Don Newcombe in the 1956 world series finale to lead the Yankees to a 9–0 victory over the Dodgers?

34) _____ Which Yankee infielder was hit in the throat by Bill Virdon's bad-hop ground ball in the 1960 world series?

35) _____ Which team was the first in history to come back from a 3–1 world series deficit in games and win the "Autumn Classic"?

36) _____ Which team was the most recent to perform the same feat?

37) _____ Who, in addition to Rogers Hornsby and Nap Lajoie, was the only right-handed batter to hit .400?

38) _____ Which Dodger catcher's throwing arm stopped the "Go-Go Sox" in the 1959 world series?

39) _____ Who lost his job as a result of Bill Mazeroski's seventh-game home run in the 1960 world series?

40) _____ Who threw the 60th home run ball to Babe Ruth in 1927?

41) _____ Who threw the 61st home run pitch to Roger Maris in 1961?

42) _____ Who was Whitey Ford's "save-ior" in 1961?

43) _____ Which of the Yankee reserve catchers hit four consecutive home runs in 1961?

44) _____ Who was the pitcher who was known as the "Yankee Killer" in the early 1960s?

45) _____ Which Hall of Famer wore the uniforms of all four New York teams: the Giants, the Dodgers, the Yankees, and the Mets?

46) _____ Which Yankee infielder was known for his "harmonica playing"?

47) _____ Which Giant pitcher once hit Johnny Roseboro with a bat?

48) _____ Whom did Sandy Koufax team up with in a joint holdout in 1966?

49) _____ Which Dodger outfielder committed three errors in one inning in the 1966 world series?

50) _____ For whom did the Reds trade Frank Robinson?

51) _____ Who was known as "Bullet Bob"?

52) _____ What position did Jackie Robinson play when he first came up with the Dodgers?

53) _____ Which former big league star is now connected with the Commissioner of Baseball's office?

54) _____ Who was the first black manager?

55) _____ Who lost three fly balls in the sun, in the same world series game for the Yankees, in 1957?

56) _____ Which Indian third baseman drove home better than 100 runs per season for five consecutive years in the early 1950s?

57) _____ Which Phillie outfielder didn't make an error during a record 266 consecutive games?

58) _____ Who was Babe Ruth's manager during his final major league season with the Boston Braves?

59) _____ Which free agent (Charley Finley style) did the Red Sox pick up in 1967 to help them win the pennant?

60) _____ Who was the last pitcher to win 30-or-more games?

61) _____ Which Brave batter was awarded first base in the 1957 world series when the black polish on the ball proved that he had been hit with the preceding pitch?

62) _____ Which Met batter was awarded first base in the same manner in the 1969 world series?

63) _____ Which Senator outfielder filed suit against baseball's reserve system in the early 1970s?

64) _____ Who was the most recent player who won the batting title without hitting a home run?

65) _____ Which second-string catcher, at the time, hit four home runs in a world series?

66) _____ Which manager resigned after leading his team to two world's championships in the 1970s?

67) _____ With what team did Leo Durocher break into the majors in 1928?

68) _____ Which 35-year-old pitcher, who had appeared in only 11 games all season long, surprised the baseball world by striking out a record 13 batters in the A's opening-game win over the Cubs in the 1929 world series?

69) _____ Which National League team once posted a .315 team batting average but finished last in the standings?

70) _____ Who won seven games and saved four others in world series play?

71) _____ Whose home run won the first All Star Game in 1933?

72) _____ What city was the only one to produce two Triple Crown winners in the same year (1933)?

73) _____ Who succeeded John McGraw as manager of the Giants?

74) _____ Which pitching brothers won 49 games in 1934?

75) _____ Whom did Commissioner Kenesaw Mountain Landis remove from the last game of the 1934 world series in order to insure the player's safety?

76) _____ Who had a career average of .439 for four world series?

77) _____ Who got the most hits in one season in the National League?

78) _____ Who stole the most bases in one season in the American League?

79) _____ Which pitcher chalked up the best winning percentage for hurlers with less than 200 but more than 100 wins?

80) _____ Who lost more games than any other pitcher in world series play?

81) _____ Who was the last Yankee player to amass 200 hits in a season?

82) _____ Who was the last Dodger player to win a home run title?

83) _____ Who was the last Yankee player to win a home run title?

84) _____ Who was the only American League player who won a batting title while splitting his time with two teams?

85) _____ Who was the only National League player who won a batting title while performing for two different teams?

86) _____ Who made nine hits in an 18-inning game?

87) _____ Which Yankee pitcher ended Mickey Cochrane's career when he felled the Tigers' playing manager with a high hard-one?

88) _____ Who was the last playing manager in the National League who led his team to a pennant?

89) _____ Which slugging Brave outfielder missed the 1948 world series—he never played in one—because of a broken ankle he sustained in a collision at home plate during the last week of the season?

90) _____ Whom did the Dodgers trade to the Pirates because he "jumped" the team on its tour of Japan after the 1966 world series?

91) _____ Which famous pitcher had to retire prematurely because of the potentially dire effects which could have been produced by his arthritic elbow?

92) _____ Who was the Commissioner of Baseball who was fired in 1968?

93) _____ Which National League manager, who was a former first baseman, was fired in August of 1938 when his team, the Cubs, was in third place? The Cubs then went on to win the pennant under Gabby Hartnett.

94) _____ Which Yankee catcher holds the major league record of handling 950 consecutive chances without making an error?

95) _____ Which Astro catcher set a major league record when he played 138 consecutive games without making an error?

96) _____ Who recorded the highest lifetime average (.358) in the history of the National League?

97) _____ Who holds the American League mark of 184 RBI in a season?

98) _____ Which two players walked 148 times in one

season to tie for the National League high in that department?

99) _____ Who recorded the most shutouts in one season in the American League?

100) _____ Whose base hit drove home the winning run for the Reds in the 1975 world series against the Red Sox?

Answers

29. From Ruth to Reggie

1) Hank Greenberg
2) Johnny Allen (1937)
3) Earl Averill
4) Monty Stratton (1938)
5) Ossie Vitt
6) Bob Feller
7) Frank Robinson
8) Hank Greenberg
9) Chris Chambliss
10) Hank Borowy
11) Phil Masi
12) Joe McCarthy
13) Hank Bauer (Kansas City, 1961)
14) Lou Boudreau (Cleveland, 1948)
15) Joe Gordon
16) Rocky Colavito
17) Stu Miller
18) Lou Boudreau
19) Ted Williams
20) Cal Abrams
21) Bobo Holloman (Browns, 1953)
22) Chuck Stobbs
23) Chuck Dressen
24) Johnny Antonelli
25) Willie Mays
26) Hank Aaron
27) Vic Wertz
28) Ruben Gomez
29) Pat Dobson
30) Tommy Byrne
31) Gil McDougald
32) Sal Maglie
33) Yogi Berra
34) Tony Kubek
35) Pirates (1925)
36) Pirates (1979)
37) Harry Heilmann (.403 in 1923)
38) Johnny Roseboro
39) Casey Stengel
40) Tom Zachary
41) Tracy Stallard
42) Luis Arroyo
43) Johnny Blanchard
44) Frank Lary
45) Casey Stengel

46) Phil Linz
47) Juan Marichal
48) Don Drysdale
49) Willie Davis
50) Milt Pappas
51) Bob Turley
52) First Base
53) Monte Irvin
54) Frank Robinson
55) Norm Siebern
56) Al Rosen
57) Don Demeter
58) Bill McKechnie
59) Ken Harrelson
60) Denny McLain
    (31–6 in 1968)
61) Nippy Jones
62) Cleon Jones
63) Curt Flood
64) Rod Carew (1972)
65) Gene Tenace
    (1972)
66) Dick Williams
67) The Yankees
68) Howard Ehmke
69) The Phillies (1930)
70) Allie Reynolds
71) Babe Ruth
72) Philadelphia
    (Jimmie Foxx, A's;
    Chuck Klein, Phil-
    lies)
73) Bill Terry
74) Jerome and Paul
    Dean
75) Joe Medwick
76) Bobby Brown
    (1947, 1949–51)
77) Lefty O'Doul (254,

1929) and Bill
Terry (254, 1930)
78) Rickey Henderson
    (100 in 1980)
79) Spud Chandler
    (.717)
80) Whitey Ford (8)
81) Bobby Richardson
    (209, 1962)
82) Duke Snider (1956)
83) Graig Nettles
    (1976)
84) David Dale Alex-
    ander (1932, Tigers
    and Red Sox)
85) Harry Walker
    (1947, Cardinals
    and Phillies)
86) Johnny Burnett
    (1932 Indians)
87) Bump Hadley
    (1937)
88) Leo Durocher
    (1941)
89) Jeff Heath
90) Maury Wills
91) Sandy Koufax
    (1966)
92) Bill Eckert
93) Charlie Grimm
94) Yogi Berra
95) Johnny Edwards
96) Rogers Hornsby
97) Lou Gehrig (1931)
98) Eddie Stanky
    (1945) and Jimmy
    Wynn (1969)
99) Jack Coombs (13,
    1910)
100) Joe Morgan

Who's on First

Going into the 1940 season, baseball experts would never have believed that the hero of the upcoming world series would be Jimmie Wilson; for the .284 lifetime hitter had recently settled down to life as a full-time coach with the Reds after donning the "tools of ignorance" for 17 seasons. But fate has been known to throw tricky pitches to a baseball team.

Ernie Lombardi, the team's regular catcher, had won the batting title two years before; he would also win it two years later. Behind him was a .316 lifetime hitter. So there didn't seem to be any need for Wilson's services.

But on August 2 the second-string catcher took his own life in Boston, and in mid-September Lombardi sprained his ankle. So Wilson was rushed back into action.

Down the stretch, "Ace" batted only .234; but he was primed up by world series time. He handled the serves of two-game winners Bucky Walters and Paul Derringer faultlessly; and he swung a torrid bat, hitting .353 in the six games he played. In addition, the 40-year-old catcher stole the only base of the entire series.

The following season, Wilson went into permanent retirement, Lombardi took over the regular catching chores once again, and the reasons for the substitute catcher's suicide remained a mystery.

The identity of that .316 lifetime hitter is pretty much a mystery, too. Can you solve it?

Answer: Willard Hershberger

Chapter Five

THE WORLD SERIES

30. WORLD SERIES STANDOUTS

I.

Match the following players with the world series records that they set: Lou Gehrig, Hank Bauer, Pee Wee Reese and Elston Howard, Yogi Berra, Eddie Mathews and Wayne Garrett, Casey Stengel, Pepper Martin, Babe Ruth, Bobby Richardson, and Mickey Mantle.

1) _____ He was on the winning club ten times.
2) _____ He was on the losing team six times.
3) _____ He was a series manager ten times.
4) _____ He hit .625, the all-time high, in one series.
5) _____ He had a career average of .418.
6) _____ He collected 12 RBI in one series.
7) _____ He hit safely in 17 consecutive games.
8) _____ He hit four home runs in four games.
9) _____ He struck out 11 times in one series.
10) _____ He struck out 54 times in series play.

II.

Match the following pitchers with the world series records they set: Bill Bevens, Whitey Ford, Harry Brecheen, Babe Ruth, Darold Knowles, Don Larsen, Christy Mathewson, Carl Mays, Bob Gibson, and Jim Palmer.

1) _____ He pitched 33 and 2/3 consecutive scoreless innings.

2) _____ He pitched seven games in one series.
3) _____ He pitched three shutouts in one series.
4) _____ He struck out 17 batters in one game.
5) _____ He issued 10 walks in one game.
6) _____ He did not allow a single walk in 26 innings of pitching in one series.
7) _____ He gave up a total of four hits in two consecutive games.
8) _____ He was the youngest pitcher who threw a shutout.
9) _____ He was the first post World War II pitcher who won three games.
10) _____ He pitched the longest game, 14 innings, which he won.

III.

Match the following teams that have won consecutive world series with the proper time spans (teams may be used more than once): Yankees, Cubs, Athletics, Giants, and Red Sox.

1) _____ (1907–08)
2) _____ (1910–11)
3) _____ (1915–16)
4) _____ (1921–22)
5) _____ (1927–28)
6) _____ (1929–30)
7) _____ (1936–39)
8) _____ (1949–53)
9) _____ (1961–62)
10) _____ (1972–74)

IV.

Match the following world series defensive standouts with the years in which they excelled: Dick Green, Tommie Agee, Willie Mays, Al Gionfriddo, Brooks Robinson,

Billy Cox, Bill Virdon, Mickey Mantle, Eddie Mathews, and Sandy Amoros.

1) _____ (1947)
2) _____ (1952)
3) _____ (1954)
4) _____ (1955)
5) _____ (1956)
6) _____ (1957)
7) _____ (1960)
8) _____ (1969)
9) _____ (1970)
10) _____ (1974)

V.

Match the following world series starting pitchers with the years in which they stood in the sun: Sandy Koufax, Lew Burdette, Mickey Lolich, Harry Brecheen, Johnny Podres, Bob Gibson, Whitey Ford, Bob Turley, Jim Hunter, and Don Larsen.

1) _____ (1946)
2) _____ (1955)
3) _____ (1956)
4) _____ (1957)
5) _____ (1958)
6) _____ (1960)
7) _____ (1963)
8) _____ (1967)
9) _____ (1968)
10) _____ (1972)

31. WORLD SERIES PLAYERS

From the performers listed below, pick out the ones who played in the world series. The key word is "played."

Richie Ashburn	Vada Pinson
Ernie Banks	Felipe Alou
Ted Williams	Jesus Alou
Al Kaline	Matty Alou
Luke Appling	Gus Bell
Mickey Vernon	Willard Marshall
Nelson Fox	Walker Cooper
Dean Chance	Ray Sadecki
Ralph Kiner	Bob Allison
Richie Allen	Vern Stephens
Harvey Kuenn	Eddie Yost
George Kell	Ferguson Jenkins
Herb Score	Satchel Paige
Hank Sauer	Johnny Callison
Johnny Logan	Buddy Kerr
Ted Kluszewski	Bill White
Bobby Murcer	Jeff Heath
Gordy Coleman	Milt Pappas
Ferris Fain	Frank Torre
Gaylord Perry	Hank Majeski

1) _____	11) _____
2) _____	12) _____
3) _____	13) _____
4) _____	14) _____
5) _____	15) _____
6) _____	16) _____
7) _____	17) _____
8) _____	18) _____
9) _____	19) _____
10) _____	20) _____

32. TWO-TEAM WORLD SERIES PLAYERS

From the performers listed below, pick out the ones who played in the world series with two different teams.

Rocky Nelson	Enos Slaughter
Juan Marichal	Don Hoak
Denny McLain	Ron Fairly
Gino Cimoli	Orlando Cepeda
Rudy York	Maury Wills
Tommy Holmes	Bob Tolan
Willie Horton	Moe Drabowsky
Bill Skowron	Joe Cronin
Roger Maris	Luis Aparicio
Al Dark	Don Gullett
George McQuinn	Dick Groat
Mickey Cochrane	Ron Perranoski
Julian Javier	Claude Osteen
Rusty Staub	Frank Robinson
Jim Lonborg	Willie Davis
Reggie Smith	Camilo Pascual
Joe Gordon	Tony Oliva
Curt Simmons	Mike Garcia
Tommy Davis	Ken Boyer
Johnny Sain	Curt Flood

1) _____   11) _____
2) _____   12) _____
3) _____   13) _____
4) _____   14) _____
5) _____   15) _____
6) _____   16) _____
7) _____   17) _____
8) _____   18) _____
9) _____   19) _____
10) _____   20) _____

33. MOUND CLASSICS

Below you will find the matchups and years in which pitchers have engaged in 1–0 mound duels since 1946. Name the winning pitcher.

1) Bob Feller vs. Johnny Sain (1948)
2) Don Newcombe vs. Allie Reynolds (1949)
3) Preacher Roe vs. Vic Raschi (1949)
4) Vic Raschi vs. Jim Konstanty (1950)
5) Bob Turley vs. Clem Labine (1956)
6) Whitey Ford vs. Lew Burdette (1957)
7) Bob Shaw, Billy Pierce, and Dick Donavan vs. Sandy Koufax (1959)
8) Ralph Terry vs. Jack Sanford (1962)
9) Jim Bouton vs. Don Drysdale (1963)
10) Claude Osteen vs. Wally Bunker (1966)
11) Don Drysdale vs. Dave McNally (1966)
12) Jack Billingham and Clay Carroll vs. John Odom (1972)

34. SEVENTH-GAME WINNERS

From the following pairs of seventh-game starting pitchers, since the end of World War II, pick the eight moundsmen who have been credited with wins. One of the eight pitchers picked up two victories.

Boo Ferriss (Red Sox) vs. Murry Dickson (Cardinals), 1946

Hal Gregg (Dodgers) vs. Frank Shea (Yankees,) 1947

Ed Lopat (Yankees) vs. Joe Black (Dodgers), 1952

Carl Erskine (Dodgers) vs. Whitey Ford (Yankees), 1953

Johnny Podres (Dodgers) vs. Tommy Byrne (Yankees), 1955

Johnny Kucks (Yankees) vs. Don Newcombe (Dodgers), 1956

Lew Burdette (Braves) vs. Don Larsen (Yankees), 1957

Don Larsen (Yankees) vs. Lew Burdette (Braves), 1958

Bob Turley (Yankees) vs. Vernon Law (Pirates), 1960

Ralph Terry (Yankees) vs. Jack Sanford (Giants), 1962

Mel Stottlemyre (Yankees) vs. Bob Gibson (Cardinals), 1964

Bob Gibson (Cardinals) vs. Jim Lonborg (Red Sox), 1967

Mickey Lolich (Tigers) vs. Bob Gibson (Cardinals), 1968

Steve Blass (Pirates) vs. Dave McNally (Orioles), 1971

John Odom (A's) vs. Jack Billingham (Reds), 1972

Jon Matlack (Mets) vs. Ken Holtzman (A's), 1973

Don Gullett (Reds) vs. Bill Lee (Red Sox), 1975

Jim Bibby (Pirates) vs. Scott McGregor (Orioles), 1979

35. WORLD SERIES SHORTS

I.

The last five pitchers who won three games in a world series were Lew Burdette, Stan Coveleski, Harry Brecheen, Mickey Lolich, and Bob Gibson. Put them in their proper order.

1) _____ (1920)
2) _____ (1946)
3) _____ (1957)
4) _____ (1967)
5) _____ (1968)

II.

Match the following players with the number of series homers they hit: Duke Snider, Mickey Mantle, Babe Ruth, Lou Gehrig, and Yogi Berra.

1) _____ (18)
2) _____ (15)
3) _____ (12)
4) _____ (11)
5) _____ (10)

III.

Match the following players with the world series records they set: Whitey Ford, Christy Mathewson, Lefty Gomez, Lefty Grove, and Bob Gibson.

1) _____ Fewest number of chances accepted (0), series (26 innings)
2) _____ Most career wins (10)

3) _____ Most strikeouts per nine innings (10.22)
4) _____ Most career shutouts (4)
5) _____ Best career-winning percentage (1.000), six decisions

IV.

Match the following players with the career world series records they set: Yogi Berra, Bobby Richardson, Frank Isbell, Dusty Rhodes, and Eddie Collins and Lou Brock.

1) _____ Tied for stolen base leadership (14)
2) _____ Most games (75)
3) _____ Most runs batted in (7) consecutive times at bat
4) _____ Most two-base hits (4), one game
5) _____ Most consecutive games played (30)

36. FOUR HOMERS IN ONE SERIES

Reggie Jackson, of course, hit five home runs in the 1977 world series. But there have been six players who hit four home runs in a series. One of them did it twice. Out of the following players pick the ones who accomplished the feat: Mickey Mantle, Willie Mays, Lou Gehrig, Gene Tenace, Roy Campanella, Joe DiMaggio, Babe Ruth, Duke Snider, Johnny Bench, and Hank Bauer, and Willie Aikens. Also, see if you can put them in their proper time spans. And, remember, one of them did it twice.

1) _____ (1926)
2) _____ (1928)
3) _____ (1952)
4) _____ (1955)
5) _____ (1958)
6) _____ (1972)

37. WORLD SERIES CHRONOLOGY

There have been 77 world series. The Autumn Classic began in 1903 and has been played every year with the exception of 1905, when the Giants refused to play the Red Sox, winners of the first series. I'm going to give you one question for each series, presented in sequence. Let's see how you know the world series—from start to finish.

1) _____ Who hit the first home run?

2) _____ Who has been the only pitcher to spin three shutouts in the same series?

3) _____ Who struck out a record 12 batters in the inter-city series between the White Sox and Cubs in 1906?

4) _____ Who was the other member of the Tinkers to Evers to Chance infield who hit .471 in 1907?

5) _____ Who was the Cub pitcher, in addition to Three Finger Brown, who won two games in 1908?

6) _____ Who has been the only rookie pitcher to win three games in one series?

7) _____ Who managed to win all three of his decisions in 1910 despite the fact that he yielded 23 hits and 14 passes?

8) _____ Who hit home runs in consecutive games for the Athletics in 1911?

9) _____ Who won three games for the Red Sox in 1912?

10) _____ Who was the only substitute whom the Athletics used in 1913?

11) _____ Who was the member of the Tinkers to Evers to Chance infield who hit .438 for the winning Braves in 1914?

12) _____ Who was the Red Sox pitcher who won two games and batted .500 in 1915?

13) _____ Who strung together the most consecutive scoreless innings in one game?

14) _____ Who was the White Sox pitcher who won three games in 1917?

15) _____ Who was the Cub second baseman who became the last out of the third game in 1918 when he unsuccessfully tried to steal home?

16) _____ Who was the untainted member of the 1919 Black Sox who won both of his decisions?

17) _____ Who hit the first grand slam?

18) _____ Who did not allow an earned run in 27 innings of pitching, but lost the final game of 1921 on an error?

19) _____ Who was the first pitcher to win the final game of two consecutive series?

20) _____ Who was the first player to hit three home runs in the same series?

21) _____ Who hit the bad-hop single that gave the Senators their first-and-only world championship?

22) _____ Who was the first pitcher to win the seventh game of one world series (1924) and lose the seventh game of the following post-season get-together?

23) _____ Who, in addition to Grover Alexander, won two games for the Cardinals in 1926?

24) _____ Who hit the only two home runs of the 1927 classic?

25) _____ Who was deprived of a "quick-pitch" strike-out of Babe Ruth in 1928?

26) _____ Who was the Athletic outfielder who, in addition to Jimmie Foxx and Mule Haas, hit two home runs in 1929?

27) _____ Who was the 46-year-old pitcher who appeared in the 1930 series?

28) _____ Who "peppered" 12 hits and swiped five bases in 1931?

29) _____ Who was the Yankee player who, in addition to Babe Ruth and Lou Gehrig, hit two home runs in one game in 1932?

30) _____ Who hit the home run in the tenth inning that won the 1933 finale?

31) _____ Who, in 1934, played on his second world championship team with one club in the 1930s after per-

forming on two world title clubs with another team in the 1920s?

32) _____ Who was the veteran outfielder whose single in 1935 gave the Tigers their first world championship?

33) _____ Who was the Giant pitcher who stopped the Yankees' 12-game win streak in 1936?

34) _____ Who was the 20-game winner for the Giants in 1937 who lost both of his series decisions?

35) _____ Who won two games during the Yankees' four-game sweep in 1938?

36) _____ Who won his fourth-and-final game (1939) without a defeat in series play?

37) _____ Who won both of his decisions, weaved a 1.50 ERA, and hit a home run in 1940?

38) _____ Who was the Dodger pitcher in 1941 who broke the Yankees' ten-game winning streak?

39) _____ Who hit a two-run homer in the final game of 1942 to give the Cardinals the world title?

40) _____ Who allowed only one run in 18 innings of pitching as the Yankees scored a turnabout five-game win over the Cardinals in 1943?

41) _____ Who was the Cardinal pitcher who lost a two-hitter to the Browns in 1944?

42) _____ Who was the starting pitcher who did not retire a single Tiger batter in Game Seven of 1945?

43) _____ Who scored the decisive run of 1946 by racing from first to home on a single?

44) _____ Who was the Dodger pitcher who finished a record six games against the Yankees in 1947?

45) _____ Who was the Indian pitcher who suffered both of his team's reversals in 1948?

46) _____ Who hit the ninth-inning home run that scored the only run in a classic duel between Allie Reynolds and Don Newcombe in the 1949 opener?

47) _____ Who was the 21-year-old rookie pitcher who won the final game in 1950?

48) _____ Who made the sliding catch that ended the 1951 series on a victorious note for the Yankees?

49) _____ Who was the Yankee part-time player who

hit a record three home runs in three consecutive games in 1952?

50) _____ Who was the Dodger pitcher who struck out a record 14 batters in one game?

51) _____ Who was the Indian slugger who hit the 450-foot fly ball that Willie Mays ran down in Game One of 1954?

52) _____ Who was the Dodger slugger who drove home both runs in Johnny Podres' 2–0 win over Tommy Byrne in Game Seven of 1955?

53) _____ Who was the 40-year-old outfielder whose three-run game-winning homer (Game Three) turned the series around for the Yankees in 1956?

54) _____ Who was the Brave pitcher of 1957 who won three games?

55) _____ Who won two of the last three games—and saved the other one—in 1958?

56) _____ Who was the former Rose Bowl performer who set a record by hitting two pinch-hit homers for the Dodgers in 1959?

57) _____ Who was the Pirate pitcher who saved three games in a winning cause in 1960?

58) _____ Who was the Yankee pitcher who won two games for the second consecutive year in 1961?

59) _____ Who was the former Yankee celebrity who defeated the Pinstripers in his only decision in 1962?

60) _____ Who was the Yankee pinch-hitter whom Sandy Koufax fanned for his record 15th strikeout in 1963?

61) _____ Who was the last runner to steal home?

62) _____ Who (in addition to Sandy Koufax, who threw two shutouts) pitched a whitewash for the Dodgers in 1965?

63) _____ Who was the only Oriole pitcher who did not complete a game in 1966?

64) _____ Who was the only Cardinal pitcher to throw three consecutive complete-game wins in a series?

65) _____ Who picked two runners off first base in the sixth inning of the final game in 1968?

66) _____ Who was the light-hitting infielder for the Mets who batted .455 in 1969?

67) _____ Who was the Oriole player who excelled in offense and defense in 1970?

68) _____ Who was the Pirate player who extended his batting streak to 14 games in 1971?

69) _____ Who was the Oakland starter who picked up his second win of the series in relief in Game Seven of 1972?

70 _____ Who outpitched Jon Matlack in both the first and last game of 1973?

71) _____ Who, in addition to Catfish Hunter, won two games for the A's in 1974?

72) _____ Who was the Red slugger who hit three home runs in 1975?

73) _____ Who was the Red slugger who batted .533 during his team's sweep of the Yankees in 1976?

74) _____ Who was the Yankee batter who extended his consecutive-game hitting streak to ten in 1977?

75) _____ Who was the Yankee fill-in infielder who batted .438 in 1978?

76) _____ Who, in addition to Willie Stargell, collected 12 hits for the Pirates in 1979?

77) _____ Who was the Phillie pitcher who won Game Five and saved Game Six in 1980?

30. World Series Standouts

I.

1) Yogi Berra
2) Pee Wee Reese, Elston Howard
3) Casey Stengel
4) Babe Ruth (1928)
5) Pepper Martin
6) Bobby Richardson
7) Hank Bauer
8) Lou Gehrig (1928)
9) Eddie Mathews, Wayne Garrett
10) Mickey Mantle

5) Yankees
6) Athletics
7) Yankees
8) Yankees
9) Yankees
10) A's.

II.

1) Whitey Ford
2) Darold Knowles
3) Christy Mathewson
4) Bob Gibson
5) Bill Bevens
6) Carl Mays
7) Jim Lonborg (1967)
8) Jim Palmer (20)
9) Harry Brecheen
10) Babe Ruth

IV.

1) Al Gionfriddo
2) Billy Cox
3) Willie Mays
4) Sandy Amoros
5) Mickey Mantle
6) Eddie Mathews
7) Bill Virdon
8) Tommie Agee
9) Brooks Robinson
10) Dick Green

V.

III.

1) Cubs
2) Athletics
3) Red Sox
4) Giants

1) Harry Brecheen
2) Johnny Podres
3) Don Larsen
4) Lew Burdette
5) Bob Turley
6) Whitey Ford
7) Sandy Koufax
8) Bob Gibson
9) Mickey Lolich
10) Jim Hunter

31. World Series Players

1) Richie Ashburn
2) Ted Williams
3) Al Kaline
4) Nelson Fox
5) Harvey Kuenn
6) Johnny Logan
7) Ted Kluszewski
8) Gordy Coleman
9) Vada Pinson
10) Felipe Alou
11) Matty Alou
12) Gus Bell
13) Walker Cooper
14) Ray Sadecki
15) Bob Allison
16) Vern Stephens
17) Satchel Paige
18) Bill White
19) Frank Torre
20) Hank Majeski

32. Two-Team World Series Players

1) Rocky Nelson (Dodgers, '52; Pirates, '60)
2) Gino Cimoli (Dodgers, '56; Pirates, '60)
3) Rudy York (Tigers, 1940, 1945; Red Sox, 1946)
4) Tommy Holmes (Braves, '48; Dodgers, '52)
5) Bill Skowron (Yankees, 1955–58, 1961–62; Dodgers, 1963)
6) Roger Maris (Yankees, 1960–64; Cardinals, 1967–68)
7) Al Dark (Braves, '48; Giants, 1951 and 1954)
8) George McQuinn (Browns, '44; Yankees, '47)
9) Mickey Cochrane (Athletics, 1929–31; Tigers, 1934–35)
10) Reggie Smith (Red Sox, '67; Dodgers, 1977–78)
11) Joe Gordon (Yankees, 1938–39, 1941–43; Indians, '48)
12) Johnny Sain (Braves, '48; Yankees, 1951–53)
13) Enos Slaughter (Cardinals, 1942, 1946; Yankees, 1956–58)
14) Don Hoak (Dodgers, 1955; Pirates, 1960)
15) Orlando Cepeda (Giants, '62; Cardinals, '67–68)
16) Bob Tolan (Cardinals, '67–68; Reds,

1970, 1972)
17) Luis Aparicio (White Sox, '59; Orioles, '66)
18) Don Gullett (Reds, 1970, 1972, 1975–

76; Yankees, 1977)
19) Dick Groat (Pirates, '60; Cardinals, '64)
20) Frank Robinson (Reds, 1961; Orioles, 1966, 1969–71)

33. Mound Classics

1) Johnny Sain
2) Allie Reynolds
3) Preacher Roe
4) Vic Raschi
5) Clem Labine
6) Lew Burdette
7) Bob Shaw
8) Ralph Terry
9) Don Drysdale
10) Wally Bunker
11) Dave McNally
12) Jack Billingham

34. Seventh-Game Winners

1) Johnny Podres
2) Johnny Kucks
3) Lew Burdette
4) Ralph Terry
5) Bob Gibson
6) Bob Gibson
7) Mickey Lolich
8) Steve Blass
9) Ken Holtzman

35. World Series Shorts

I.

1) Stan Coveleski
2) Harry Brecheen
3) Lew Burdette
4) Bob Gibson
5) Mickey Lolich

II.

1) Mickey Mantle
2) Babe Ruth
3) Yogi Berra
4) Duke Snider
5) Lou Gehrig

III.

1) Lefty Grove
2) Whitey Ford
3) Bob Gibson
4) Christy Mathewson
5) Lefty Gomez

IV.

1) Eddie Collins,
   Lou Brock

2) Yogi Berra
3) Dusty Rhodes (He batted in 7 runs in four consecutive at-bats for the Giants in 1954.)
4) Frank Isbell
5) Bobby Richardson

36. Four Homers in One Series

1) Babe Ruth
2) Lou Gehrig
3) Duke Snider
4) Duke Snider
5) Hank Bauer
6) Gene Tenace
7) Willie Aikens

37. World Series Chronology

1) Jimmy Sebring (Pirates)
2) Christy Mathewson
3) Ed Walsh (White Sox)
4) Harry Steinfeldt
5) Orval Overall
6) Babe Adams
7) Jack Coombs (Athletics)
8) Frank Baker
9) Joe Wood
10) Jack Lapp
11) Johnny Evers
12) George "Rube" Foster
13) Babe Ruth (13⅓)
14) Red Faber
15) Charlie Pick
16) Dickie Kerr
17) Elmer Smith (Indians)
18) Waite Hoyt (Yankees)
19) Art Nehf
20) Babe Ruth
21) Earl McNeely
22) Walt Johnson
23) Jesse Haines
24) Babe Ruth
25) Bill Sherdel
26) Al Simmons

27) Jack Quinn
28) Pepper Martin
29) Tony Lazzeri
30) Mel Ott
31) Frankie Frisch
32) Goose Goslin
33) Carl Hubbell
34) Cliff Melton
35) Red Ruffing
36) Monte Pearson
37) Bucky Walters
38) Whit Wyatt
39) Whitey Kurowski
40) Spud Chandler
41) Mort Cooper
42) Hank Borowy
43) Enos Slaughter
44) Hugh Casey
45) Bob Feller
46) Tommy Henrich
47) Whitey Ford
48) Hank Bauer
49) Johnny Mize
50) Carl Erskine
51) Vic Wertz
52) Gil Hodges
53) Enos Slaughter
54) Lew Burdette

53) Enos Slaughter
54) Lew Burdette
55) Bob Turley
56) Chuck Essegian
57) Roy Face
58) Whitey Ford
59) Don Larsen
60) Harry Bright
61) Tim McCarver
    (Cardinals)
62) Claude Osteen
63) Dave McNally
    (Game One)
64) Bob Gibson
65) Mickey Lolich
66) Al Weis
67) Brooks Robinson
68) Roberto Clemente
69) Jim Hunter
70) Ken Holtzman
71) Ken Holtzman
72) Tony Perez
73) Johnny Bench
74) Thurman Munson
75) Brian Doyle
76) Phil Garner
77) Tug McGraw

Who's on First

What's happened to the complete game in world series play?

Why, in the first world series (1903) that was ever played, a Pirate strong man pitched five complete games. That's right, it's still a record. But, in that same series, a rubber arm for the Red Sox pitched four complete games. That's the second highest number of complete games that has ever been pitched in one series.

As recently as 1956, though, five different Yankee pitchers threw complete games in consecutive contests. They were Whitey Ford, Tom Sturdivant, Don Larsen, Bob Turley, and Johnny Kucks, respectively. That's a record, too.

They must not make them the way they used to, though. Take the National League, for example. In the 1970s, 61 world series games were played. But National League pitchers threw only five complete games. (And one of the pitchers hurled full games twice.) That's a complete-game average of 8.2 per cent.

During the 1970s, 29 different pitchers in the National League started a game. Some of them did it a number of times. But only four of those 29 pitchers managed to complete a game. That's a pitcher-completion average of 13.8 per cent.

National League pitchers began the decade by failing to get a complete game out of the first seven starters. In 1971 two different pitchers completed three games. But from 1972 to Game Two of the 1977 series, Senior Circuit hurlers failed to complete a game in 31 attempts. Two different pitchers completed games for the National League representative in 1977. But Chub Feeney's league is on another streak: in the last 18 games the National League has not gotten a route-going performance from one of its starters.

If you can name two of the four complete-game pitchers, you're already doing better than the National League hurlers of the 1970s did. If you can name three of them, you can take your turn with Ford, Kucks, *et al.* If you can come up with four of the pitchers, Bill Dinneen of the 1903 Red Sox will have to move over in order to make room for you. And if you can spiel off all four pitchers, including the one pitcher who did it twice, you and Deacon Phillippe of the 1903 Pirates are in a class by yourselves.

Answer: The pitchers are Steve Blass and Nelson Briles of the 1971 Pirates and Burt Hooton and Don Sutton of the 1977 Dodgers. Blass recorded the two complete games.

Chapter Six

THE MANAGERS

38. QUICK QUIZZING THE MANAGERS

I.

From the names listed in the right-hand column, list in order: 1) the youngest manager ever to begin a season, 2) the youngest manager ever to finish a season, 3) the youngest manager ever to win a pennant, 4) the oldest manager ever to debut as manager, and 5) the oldest manager ever to win a pennant for the first time.

1) _____ Roger Peckinpaugh
2) _____ Tom Sheehan
3) _____ Burt Shotton
4) _____ Joe Cronin
5) _____ Lou Boudreau

II.

Match the successful managers listed on the right-hand side with the number of pennants and World Series (combined total) they won. The total is contained in parentheses on the left-hand side.

1) _____ (17) Walter Alston
2) _____ (16) Casey Stengel
3) _____ (14) John McGraw
4) _____ (13) Joe McCarthy
5) _____ (11) Connie Mack

III.

The men listed on the left-hand side were all playing managers who won at least one pennant. Yet each was traded—while still a player on that team—to another one which, in every case but one, the player continued to manage. Match the playing manager with the trade in which he was connected.

1) _____ Joe Cronin a) Indians–Red Sox
2) _____ Rogers Hornsby b) Senators–Tigers
3) _____ Lou Boudreau c) Cardinals–Giants
4) _____ Bucky Harris d) Cubs–Yankees
5) _____ Frank Chance e) Senators–Red Sox

IV.

Match the managers in the right-hand column with their respective all-time winning percentages in the left-hand column.

1) _____ (.614) Billy Southworth
2) _____ (.593) Frank Chance
3) _____ (.593) John McGraw
4) _____ (.589) Joe McCarthy
5) _____ (.582) Al Lopez

39. DID THEY OR DIDN'T THEY...
MANAGE?

When we look back, we sometimes find it hard to sort out fact from fiction in baseball. See if you can zero in on the twenty players who became managers from the following list of forty.

Joe Adcock	Red Rolfe
Bobby Brown	Roy Smalley
Joe Gordon	Duke Snider
Ken Keltner	Ben Chapman
Enos Slaughter	Jim Landis
Kerby Farrell	Jim Lemon
Bill Dickey	Jerry Lynch
Bucky Walters	Freddie Fitzsimmons
Bobby Wine	Irv Noren
Eddie Pellagrini	Wally Post
Del Rice	Bob Elliott
Nippy Jones	Eddie Lopat
Phil Cavarretta	Jerry Priddy
Christy Mathewson	Gene Hermanski
Sid Hudson	Babe Ruth
Bob Friend	Johnny Pesky
Bobby Thomson	Jim Hegan
Luke Appling	Dick Sisler
Eddie Joost	Mel McGaha
Mickey Vernon	Eddie Stanky

1) _____	11) _____
2) _____	12) _____
3) _____	13) _____
4) _____	14) _____
5) _____	15) _____
6) _____	16) _____
7) _____	17) _____
8) _____	18) _____
9) _____	19) _____
10) _____	20) _____

40. POST-WAR WORLD SERIES WINNERS

There have been 22 managers who have led their teams to world series victories in the post World War II era. Eleven of them have been National League managers; eleven of them have been American League skippers. See how many of them you can name.

41. BACK-TO-BACK PENNANT WINNERS

There have been 11 major league managers in the post World War II era who have led their teams to consecutive pennants. Two of them have done it twice. See if you can place the name with the period.

1) _____ (1949–53)
2) _____ (1952–53)
3) _____ (1955–56)
4) _____ (1955–58)*
5) _____ (1957–58)
6) _____ (1961–63)
7) _____ (1965–66)*
8) _____ (1967–68)
9) _____ (1969–71)
10) _____ (1972–73)
11) _____ (1975–76)
12) _____ (1976–77)
13) _____ (1977–78)

* The second time.

42. MANAGERS IN SEARCH OF A PENNANT

Name the ten managers from the following 20 who never led a team to the pennant: Red Rolfe, Steve O'Neill, Eddie Stanky, Bill Rigney, Al Dark, Birdie Tebbetts, Fred Hutchinson, Al Lopez, Mike Higgins, Bobby Bragan, Danny Murtaugh, Harry Walker, Mel Ott, Sam Mele, Hank Bauer, Fred Haney, Johnny Keane, Gene Mauch, Dick Williams, and Paul Richards.

1) ———
2) ———
3) ———
4) ———
5) ———
6) ———
7) ———
8) ———
9) ———
10) ———

43. YOU'RE HIRED TO BE FIRED

In the left-hand column are listed men who managed 16 different major league clubs. To their right is noted the team that they managed (many of them guided more than one) and the year in which they were succeeded by a manager who started the season with his team. This eliminates interim managers who finished up a season while their owners were looking for full-time field leaders. Some of the managers who are listed were fired, some resigned, and one died. Match them with their successors who are listed in the right-hand column.

1) _____ Joe McCarthy
   (Yanks, '47)   a) Burt Shotton
2) _____ Yogi Berra   b) Bill Terry
   (Yanks, '65)   c) Leo Durocher
3) _____ John McGraw,   d) Dick Sisler
   (Giants, '33   e) Bucky Harris
4) _____ Mel Ott   f) Bobby Bragan
   (Giants, '49)*   g) Johnny Keane
5) _____ Leo Durocher   h) Eddie Dyer
   (Dodgers, '49)*   i) Walt Alston
6) _____ Charlie Dressen   j) Gene Mauch
   (Dodgers, '54)   k) Whitey Lockman
7) _____ Billy Southworth   l) Harry Walker
   (Cards, '46)   m) Red Schoendienst
8) _____ Johnny Keane   n) Earl Weaver
   (Cards, '65)   o) Al Lopez
9) _____ Eddie Sawyer   p) Al Dark
   (Phils, '61)   q) Kerby Farrell
10) _____ Danny Murtaugh   r) Joe McCarthy
    (Pirates, '65)   s) Rogers Hornsby
11) _____ Fred Hutchinson   t) Billy Martin
    (Reds, '65)
12) _____ Leo Durocher (Cubs,
    '73)

13) _____ Birdie Tebbetts
   (Braves, '63)
14) _____ Al Lopez
   (Indians, '57)
15) _____ Mayo Smith
   (Tigers, '71)
16) _____ Dick Williams
   (A's, '74)
17) _____ Zack Taylor
   (Browns, '52)
18) _____ Marty Marion
   (White Sox, '57)
19) _____ Joe Cronin
   (Red Sox, '48)
20) _____ Hank Bauer
   (Orioles, '69)

* These managers were involved in two shake-ups by team organizations shortly into the season.

44. MANAGERIAL HALF TRUTHS

Mark "T" or "F" for "True" or "False" before each statement.

1) _____ Joe Cronin was the last Red Sox manager to direct the Bosox to a world series victory.

2) _____ Joe Cronin was the last Senator manager to win a pennant.

3) _____ Lou Boudreau was the last Indian manager to win a world series.

4) _____ Bill Carrigan (1915–16) has been the only Red Sox manager to direct Boston to back-to-back world championships.

5) _____ Del Baker was the first bench manager to guide the Tigers to a pennant (1940).

6) _____ Mickey Cochrane has been the only Tiger manager to guide the Bengals to back-to-back pennants.

7) _____ Bill Rigney was the last Giant manager to lead his charges to a pennant.

8) _____ Bill Dickey never managed the Yankees.

9) _____ Chuck Dressen was the last manager to win back-to-back pennants (1952–53) with the Dodgers.

10) _____ Walter Alston has been the only manager to lead the Dodgers to the world championship.

11) _____ Leo Durocher's tenure as manager of the Dodgers was longer than his reign as boss of the Giants.

12) _____ Charlie Grimm never managed a world series winner.

13) _____ Frank Chance was the only manager of the Cubs who has won a world championship.

14) _____ Eddie Dyer, Johnny Keane, and Red Schoendienst have led the Cardinals to world titles in the post World War II era.

15) _____ Frankie Frisch was a retired player when the Cardinals won the pennant and world series in 1934.

16) _____ Al Lopez was the most recent manager who has won pennants with two different clubs.

17) _____ Fred Haney directed the Braves to their first world title in 1957.

18) _____ Bucky Harris was the only Senator manager to lead his team to two pennants.

19) _____ Bucky Harris was the youngest manager to lead his team to a world title.

20) _____ Gil Hodges had a losing record as a major league manager.

21) _____ Rogers Hornsby never managed in the American League.

22) _____ Ralph Houk won pennants in his first three years as manager of the Yankees.

23) _____ Miller Huggins won more world series than he lost.

24) _____ Fred Hutchinson never managed a pennant winner.

25) _____ Hughie Jennings of the Tigers (1907–09) was the only manager to lose three consecutive world series.

26) _____ Fielder Jones of the White Sox was the winning manager in the only inter-city world series in Chicago.

27) _____ Johnny Keane was the last Cardinal manager to lead the Redbirds to the world title.

28) _____ Al Lopez, in his first nine years of managing (1951–59), never brought his teams home worse than second.

29) _____ Connie Mack's teams won nine pennants, but they appeared in only eight world series.

30) _____ Gene Mauch managed the last pennant winner for the Phillies.

31) _____ Joe McCarthy had a better world series winning percentage with the Yankees than Casey Stengel.

32) _____ John McGraw lost more world series than any other team leader.

33) _____ Bill McKechnie was the only Red manager to lead his team to two consecutive pennants.

34) _____ Walter Alston was the only National League manager to lead his team to more than one pennant in the 1960s.

35) _____ Walter Alston's managerial opponent in the 1965 world series was Sam Mele.

36) _____ Danny Murtaugh was the only Pirate manager to lead his team to the world title.

37) _____ Steve O'Neill was the last Tiger manager to lead the Bengals to the world championship.

38) _____ Wilbert Robinson won more pennants with the Dodgers than Leo Durocher.

39) _____ Billy Martin led two different teams to pennants.

40) _____ Red Schoendienst won more consecutive pennants as manager of the Cardinals than any other Redbird leader.

41) _____ Luke Sewell was the only Brown manager to lead his team to a pennant.

42) _____ Bob Shawkey and Johnny Keane were the only non-interim Yankee managers who have not won a pennant for the Pinstripers since 1918.

43) _____ Mayo Smith's 1968 Tigers were the first team to defeat the Cardinals in the world series since Joe McCarthy's 1943 Yankees.

44) _____ Billy Southworth won pennants with two different National League teams.

45) _____ Tris Speaker never managed a world series winner.

46) _____ Earl Weaver has a winning record in world series play.

47) _____ Bill Terry's managerial opponent in the 1933 series (Giants–Senators) was Bucky Harris.

48) _____ Hank Bauer led a team to a world series sweep.

49) _____ Rogers Hornsby won more games than he lost in world series play.

50) _____ Luke Appling, Ted Lyons, and Jimmy Dykes all managed the White Sox.

Answers

38. Quick Quizzing the Managers

I.

1) Lou Boudreau (24)
2) Roger Peckinpaugh (23)
3) Joe Cronin (26)
4) Tom Sheehan (66)
5) Burt Shotton (62)

II.

1) Casey Stengel
2) Joe McCarthy
3) Connie Mack
4) John McGraw
5) Walter Alston

III.

1) e
2) c
3) a
4) b
5) d

IV.

1) Joe McCarthy
2) Frank Chance or Billy Southworth
3) Frank Chance or Billy Southworth
4) John McGraw
5) Al Lopez

39. Did They or Didn't They . . . Manage?

1) Joe Adcock
2) Joe Gordon
3) Kerby Farrell
4) Bill Dickey
5) Bucky Walters
6) Phil Cavarretta
7) Christy Mathewson
8) Luke Appling
9) Eddie Joost
10) Mickey Vernon
11) Red Rolfe
12) Ben Chapman
13) Jim Lemon
14) Freddie Fitzsimmons
15) Bob Elliott
16) Eddie Lopat
17) Johnny Pesky
18) Dick Sisler
19) Mel McGaha
20) Eddie Stanky

40. Post-War World Series Winners

I. National League

1) Eddie Dyer
2) Leo Durocher
3) Walter Alston
4) Fred Haney
5) Danny Murtaugh
6) Johnny Keane
7) Red Schoendienst
8) Gil Hodges
9) Sparky Anderson
10) Chuck Tanner

II. American League

1) Bucky Harris
2) Lou Boudreau
3) Casey Stengel
4) Ralph Houk
5) Hank Bauer
6) Mayo Smith
7) Earl Weaver
8) Dick Williams
9) Al Dark
10) Billy Martin
11) Bob Lemon

41. Back-to-Back Pennant Winners

1) Casey Stengel
2) Chuck Dressen
3) Walter Alston
4) Casey Stengel
5) Fred Haney
6) Ralph Houk
7) Walter Alston
8) Red Schoendienst
9) Earl Weaver
10) Dick Williams
11) Sparky Anderson
12) Billy Martin
13) Tom LaSorda

42. Managers in Search of a Pennant

1) Red Rolfe
2) Eddie Stanky
3) Bill Rigney
4) Birdie Tebbetts
5) Mike Higgins
6) Bobby Bragan
7) Harry Walker
8) Mel Ott
9) Gene Mauch
10) Paul Richards

43. You're Hired to be Fired

1) e
2) g
3) b
4) c

5) a	13) f
6) i	14) q
7) h	15) t
8) m	16) p
9) j	17) s
10) l	18) o
11) d	19) r
12) k	20) n

44. Managerial Half Truths

1) F (Ed Barrow, 1918)
2) T (1933)
3) T (1948)
4) T
5) T
6) F (Hughie Jennings, 1907–09)
7) F (Al Dark, 1962)
8) F (1946, as an interim skipper)
9) F (Walter Alston, 1955–56, and 1965–66)
10) T
11) T (8½ years to 7½ years)
12) T
13) T (1907–08)
14) T
15) F (He was the playing manager.)
16) F (Al Dark: Giants, 1962; and A's, 1974)
17) F (George Stallings, 1914)
18) T (1924–25)
19) T (27)

20) T (660–754)
21) F (The Browns, 1933–37 and 1952)
22) T (1961–63)
23) F (3–3)
24) F (The 1961 Reds)
25) F (John McGraw of the 1911–13 Giants, also)
26) T
27) F (Red Schoendienst, 1967)
28) T
29) T (In 1902, when he won a pennant, the world series had not yet been established.)
30) F (Eddie Sawyer, 1950)
31) T (.875–700)
32) T (6)
33) F (Sparky Anderson did it, too.)
34) F (Red Schoendienst, in 1967–68, did it, also.)
35) T
36) F (Fred Clarke,

1909; Bill McKechnie, 1925; and Chuck Tanner, 1979)

37) F (Mayo Smith, 1968)
38) T (2–1)
39) F (The 1976–77 Yankees)
40) F (Billy Southworth, 1942–44)
41) T (1944)
42) F (Bill Virdon, in 1974–75, and Dick Howser, in 1980, didn't, either.)
43) T
44) T (Cardinals, 1942–44; Braves, 1948)
45) F (The 1920 Indians)
46) F (1–3)
47) F (Joe Cronin)
48) T (The 1966 Orioles)
49) T (He was 4–3 in 1926, his only series as a manager.)
50) F (Appling did not.)

Who's on First

The Giants of John McGraw had much good fortune—they won ten pennants and three world series—but they had great misfortune, also: they lost one pennant and three world series that they could have won.

In 1908 they were victimized by "Merkle's Boner." On September 23, in a key game with the Cubs at the Polo Grounds, Al Bridwell lined a safe ball to the outfield that chased Moose McCormick home with the apparent winning run. But Merkle, who was on first, did not run out the hit to second. Instead he bolted straight to the clubhouse in center field, a custom of the time when the winning hit was made in the bottom of the ninth inning. Johnny Evers, the Cubs' second baseman, alertly called for the ball; and Hank O'Day, the umpire who saw the entire play, ruled that Merkle was out. He also suspended the 1–1 contest because of darkness. That necessitated a one-game playoff for the pennant. The Cubs behind Mordecai Brown defeated Christy Mathewson of the Giants, 4–2.

In 1912 the Giants muffed the world series. Leading by one run in the final inning of the eighth-and-decisive game—the second game had ended in a 6–6 tie—they made two costly errors, one of commission and one of omission. Fred Snodgrass dropped Clyde Engle's routine fly ball for a two-base error, and first baseman Merkle and catcher Chief Meyers gave Tris Speaker a second life when they permitted his easy foul pop to drop untouched. Speaker then singled home the tying run and advanced what proved to be the winning run to third. Larry Gardner's sacrifice fly clinched the championship.

In 1917 the Giants made two physical errors and one mental error in the fourth inning of the sixth-and-final game. Heinie Zimmerman, the third basemen for the Giants, made a bad throw on an easy grounder; Dave Robertson, the right fielder, dropped an easy fly ball; and

Bill Rariden, the catcher, left home plate unattended in a rundown play that led to the winning run.

In 1924, McGraw's last chance to win a world series, the "Little Napoleon" saw fate intervene once again. In the bottom of the twelfth, with the score between the Giants and the host Senators tied at three, Muddy Ruel lifted a high foul behind the plate; but the Giant catcher tripped over his own mask, and Ruel, given another opportunity, doubled. Earl McNeely's hopper to third hit a pebble and bounced over Fred Lindstrom's head, scoring Ruel with the winning run.

The Giants' receiver was naturally distraught over his inability to handle Ruel's pop fly properly, for he was a veteran who was used to crisis situations. Up until that time he had been the only catcher to be on the winning side of a world series sweep. When World War I erupted, he was the first major leaguer to volunteer for military service. Later, when World War II broke out, he became the only major leaguer to see service in both wars. And in the 1914 world series he batted .545, the second highest average in the history of the Autumn Classic.

Who was this player with the checkered career?

Answer: Hank Gowdy

Chapter Seven.

BASEBALL'S WHO'S WHO

45. BASEBALL'S WHO'S WHO

1) _____ Who pitched in 65 1–0 games, winning 38 of them and losing 27, even though in 20 of his losses he allowed four or fewer hits?

2) _____ Who batted for a .403 average over a five-year period of time?

3) _____ Who was the only manager to win pennants with three different teams?

4) _____ Who was the youngest player to win a batting title?

5) _____ Who was the oldest player to win a batting title?

6) _____ Who was the first player to hit safely in 12 consecutive official at-bats?

7) _____ Who was the only other player to duplicate the feat?

8) _____ Who hit .382 in his last year (570 at-bats) in the majors?

9) _____ Who was the only other player to bat .400 without winning the hitting crown?

10) _____ Who posted the most wins (12) in one season without losing a game?

11) _____ Who pitched three doubleheaders in one month and won all six games, none of which lasted more than one hour and fifty minutes?

12) _____ Who hit two game-winning home runs for the Giants against the Yankees in the 1923 series?

13) _____ Who was the only player to win the MVP award for two teams in the same league?

14) _____ Who was the first infielder to wear glasses?

15) _____ Who was the first catcher to wear glasses?

16) _____ Who was the National League right hander who led the circuit in strikeouts for four consecutive years (1932–35), but failed to whiff as many as 200 batters in a season?

17) _____ Who recorded the lowest career ERA in the world series?

18) _____ Who won four batting titles in alternate years?

19) _____ Who won back-to-back batting titles three times?

20) _____ Who was the first baseman who teamed with Joe Gordon, Lou Boudreau, and Ken Keltner to give the Indians an infield that averaged 108 RBI?

21) _____ Who was the one-time Yankee manager who neither hit a home run nor stole a base in eight major league seasons?

22) _____ Who was the one-time Yankee manager who never finished worse than fourth in 24 years as a major league skipper?

23) _____ Who was the pennant-winning manager who needed the most time—10 years—to win his first league title?

24) _____ Who hit a record six pinch-hit home runs in one year?

25) _____ Who hit five pinch-hit home runs in one year to set an American League record?

26) _____ Who was the only National League pitcher to lead his league in winning percentage for three consecutive years?

27) _____ Who was the only American League pitcher to lead his circuit in winning percentage for three consecutive years?

28) _____ Who shut out every team in the National League in three different years?

29) _____ Who was the left-handed slugger in the National League who tied for the home run title three times?

30) _____ Who was the right-handed slugger in the National League who tied for the home run crown three times?

31) _____ Who posted a 6–0 opening day record?

32) _____ Who pitched six opening day shutouts?

33) _____ Who was the only White Sox player to win a batting title?

34) _____ Who threw the pennant-winning home run to Chris Chambliss in 1976?

35) _____ Who was the only pitcher to win back-to-back MVP awards?

36) _____ Who was the pitcher for the 1914 pennant-winning Athletics who recorded a .302 lifetime mark as an outfielder?

37) _____ Who hit 40-or-more home runs in the American League eight times, but never reached the 50 mark?

38) _____ Who hit 40-or-more home runs in the National League eight times, but failed to hit the 50 mark?

39) _____ Who was the player who led the American League in batting in 1961 with an average of .361, but never before or after reached the .300 level?

40) _____ Who drove home 106 runs in 1969, at the age of 38, to become the oldest player to deliver that many ribbies?

41) _____ Who was the 273-game winner who hit over .300 eight times and pinch-hit safely 58 times?

42) _____ Who was the pitcher who pinch-hit safely 114 times?

43) _____ Who set a major league record by leading his league in ERA percentage eight times?

44) _____ Who was the only player to win the batting and home run titles with two teams in the same league?

45) _____ Who were the only pitching brothers to throw no-hitters?

46) _____ Who was the National League relief pitcher who recorded the most career saves in the Senior Circuit?

47) _____ Who was the player who three times won the batting crown and the home run title in the same year?

48) _____ Who finished 750 of 816 contests for a completion percentage of 92?

49) _____ Who was the only National League player to twice get six hits in six at-bats?

50) _____ Who was the only American League player to twice get six hits in six at-bats?

51) _____ Who was the only American League pitcher to win the Cy Young Award three times?

52) _____ Who, in addition to Sandy Koufax and Steve Carlton, was the only National League pitcher to win the Cy Young Award three times?

53) _____ Who was the first National League relief pitcher to win the Cy Young Award?

54) _____ Who was the only American League relief pitcher to win the Cy Young Award?

55) _____ Who was the only pitcher to win the Cy Young Award in both leagues?

56) _____ Who was the only American League pitcher to win the Rookie of the Year Award in the 1970s?

57) _____ Who was the only National League infielder who won the Rookie of the Year Award in the 1970s?

58) _____ Who, except Rod Carew, was the last American League hitter to win consecutive batting crowns?

59) _____ Who has been the only player to win both the Rookie of the Year Award and the MVP Award in the same year?

60) _____ Who was the last National League player to win three consecutive batting titles?

61) _____ Who was the last American League player to win at least three consecutive batting titles?

62) _____ Who was the second-and-most-recent National League relief pitcher to win the Cy Young Award?

63) _____ Who was the last National League player to win three consecutive home run crowns?

64) _____ Who was the last American League player to win back-to-back MVP awards?

65) _____ Who was the last National League player to win back-to-back MVP awards?

66) _____ Who was the only other National League player to win back-to-back MVP awards?

67) _____ Who has hit for the highest average in the National League since Stan Musial's .376 in 1948?

68) _____ Who strayed 200-or-more hits in a record ten seasons?

69) _____ Who is the present-day pitcher who once won 20-or-more games in six consecutive seasons?

70) _____ Who is the present-day pitcher who has won 20-or-more games with three different teams?

71) _____ Who is the present-day pitcher who has won 20-or-more games the most times?

72) _____ Who is the only present-day left-handed pitcher to strike out 300 batters in a season?

73) _____ Who is the present-day pitcher who holds the American League record for saves?

74) _____ Who was the most recent pitcher to both win and lose 20 games in the same season?

75) _____ Who is the present-day player who holds the club batting mark lead with two different teams?

76) _____ Who is the present-day pitcher who struck out more than 200 batters in nine consecutive seasons?

Answers

45. Baseball's Who's Who

1) Walter Johnson
2) Rogers Hornsby (1921–25)
3) Bill McKechnie (Pirates, '25; Cardinals, '28; and Reds, '39–'40)
4) Al Kaline of the Tigers, who was 20 in 1955
5) Ted Williams of the Red Sox, who was 40 in 1958
6) Mike Higgins of the 1938 Red Sox
7) Walt Dropo of the 1952 Tigers
8) Joe Jackson (1920)
9) Ty Cobb, whose .401 for the Tigers in 1922 finished second to George Sisler's .420
10) Tom Zachary of the 1929 Yankees
11) "Iron Man" Joe McGinnity of the 1903 Giants
12) Casey Stengel
13) Jimmie Foxx (A's, '32–'33; and Red Sox, '38)
14) George "Specs" Toporcer of the 1921 Cardinals
15) Clint Courtney of the 1951 Yankees
16) Dizzy Dean
17) Harry Brecheen (0.83) of the Cardinals
18) Harry Heilmann of the 1921, 1923, 1925, and 1927 Tigers
19) Ted Williams of the 1941–42, 1947–48, and 1957–58 Red Sox
20) Eddie Robinson (1948)
21) Ralph Houk
22) Joe McCarthy
23) Casey Stengel
24) Johnny Frederick of the 1932 Dodgers
25) Joe Cronin of the 1943 Red Sox
26) Ed Reulbach of the 1906–08 Cubs
27) Lefty Grove of the 1929–31 Athletics
28) Grover Alexander
29) Mel Ott of the 1932, 1934, and 1937 Giants

30) Ralph Kiner of the 1947–48, and 1952 Pirates

31) Wes Ferrell

32) Walter Johnson

33) Luke Appling (1936 and 1943)

34) Mark Littell

35) Hal Newhouser (1944–45)

36) Rube Bressler

37) Harmon Killebrew

38) Hank Aaron

39) Norm Cash

40) Ernie Banks

41) Red Ruffing

42) Red Lucas

43) Lefty Grove

44) Jimmie Foxx: batting, 1933 (Athletics) and 1938 (Red Sox); home runs, 1932–33, 1935 (Athletics) and 1939 (Red Sox).

45) Bob Forsch (Cardinals) and Ken Forsch (Astros)

46) Roy Face (193)

47) Ted Williams (1941 –42 and 1947)

48) Cy Young

49) Jim Bottomley

50) Roger Cramer

51) Jim Palmer of the 1973, 1975–76 Orioles

52) Tom Seaver of the 1969, 1973, 1975 Mets

53) Mike Marshall of the 1974 Dodgers

54) Sparky Lyle of the 1977 Yankees

55) Gaylord Perry (Indians, '72; Padres, '78)

56) Mark Fidrych of the 1976 Tigers

57) Bob Horner of the 1978 Braves

58) Carl Yastrzemski of the 1967–68 Red Sox

59) Fred Lynn of the 1975 Red Sox

60) Stan Musial of the 1950–52 Cardinals

61) Rod Carew of the 1972–75 Twins

62) Bruce Sutter (1979)

63) Mike Schmidt of the 1974–76 Phillies

64) Roger Maris of the 1960–61 Yankees

65) Joe Morgan of the 1975–76 Reds

66) Ernie Banks of the 1958–59 Cubs

67) Rico Carty, who hit .366 for the Braves in 1970

68) Pete Rose

69) Ferguson Jenkins of the 1967–72 Cubs

70) Gaylord Perry of the Giants, Indians, and Padres

71) Jim Palmer (8) of the Orioles

72) Steve Carlton (310) of the 1972 Phillies

73) Sparky Lyle (215)

74) Phil Niekro (21–20) of the 1979 Braves
75) Rusty Staub (.333) of the 1967 Astros

and (.311) of the 1971 Expos

76 Tom Seaver of the 1968–76 Mets

Who's on First

They say that good things come in twos. That goes for no-hitters, too.

There have been four pitchers in the modern era to throw two no-hitters in one season: Johnny Vander Meer (1938), Allie Reynolds (1951), Virgil Trucks (1952), and Nolan Ryan (1973). One of them (Vander Meer) was the only pitcher to throw two no-hitters in successive starts.

Up until 1968, however, no two teams had exchanged no-hitters on successive days. Now it's been accomplished twice. The first time, on September 23, 1968, a Giant pitcher performed the feat against the visiting Cardinals. The following day, a St. Louis right hander duplicated the feat against San Francisco.

One year later, two teams traded no-hitters on successive days for the second time. On April 30 a strong-armed Cincinnati right hander set back the Astros. The next day an Astro flamethrower returned the favor.

If you could name just two of the four pitchers who were involved in these classic comebacks, you would be pitching in coveted company, too. Can you?

Answer: Gaylord Perry (Giants) and Ray Washburn (Cardinals); Jim Maloney (Reds) and Don Wilson (Astros)

Chapter Eight

BASEBALL'S NUMBER GAME

Just how trivial is baseball "trivia"?

Baseball fans, the most record conscious of all sports followers, feel very strongly that names and numbers are a vital part of the National Pastime. So do the players.

The numbers 56, 60, 61, 367, 511, 755, and 2,130 instantaneously draw to the minds of astute baseball fans and players the names of great diamond stars of the past: Joe DiMaggio, Babe Ruth, Roger Maris, Ty Cobb, Cy Young, Hank Aaron, and Lou Gehrig.

Numbers 300 and 3,000 probably hold the most lure for the baseball fan and player. Three hundred represents a batter's season's average and his career mark. It also signifies a pitcher's season's strikeouts and career wins. Three thousand can stand for either career hits by a batter or career strikeouts by a pitcher.

There are other magical numbers in baseball, too. Quite often they affect the longevity of a player's career.

Mickey Mantle, the great Yankee switch-hitter, lengthened his career two years because of the numbers game. In 1966, when he should have retired, Mantle's RBI total dipped to 56. But his batting average of .288 and his home run total of 23 were still respectable. It would have been a good time to bow out: while he was still on top. But he was just four home runs shy of 500. The temptation was simply too great. So he played another year. In 1967 he hit 22 home runs to up his total to 518, just three short of Ted Williams' 521 and 16 light of Jimmy Foxx's 534. So, of course, he played one more year, and he ended up with 536 home runs. Willie Mays's four-base total, the next rung on the home run ladder, was high above Mantle's. So, with no more numbers to catch, he retired.

The numbers game was costly to Mantle, though. His .245 and .237 batting averages during his last two years dragged his lifetime average down from .302 to .298. In Mantle's case a higher home run total was preferable to a higher lifetime batting average.

"It really bothers me that I didn't end up my career with a .300 lifetime average," Mantle says when he is asked about his decision to play those last two years. "I'd like to be remembered as a good hitter. At the time I fooled myself into thinking that I could hit the extra home runs and keep the .300 average. But it didn't work out."

Al Kaline got caught up in the numbers game, too. His situation was similar to Mantle's. He played two extra years in order to wind up in the select 3,000 Hit Club. He made it with a herculean effort in 1974, when he got 146 hits to finish up his career with 3,007. But, in those last two years, he slipped four points, from .301 to .297, in his lifetime average.

Once Kaline reached 3,000 hits, he was faced with another dilemma. He had 399 home runs. Should he play another year in order to end up in another select circle of hitters: the 400 Home Run Club?

"No, I decided not to," Kaline said shortly after his retirement. "It would have been nice to hit 400 home runs. But the toll that would have been exacted from my body, by playing another season, would have been too much. I had a good career. I'm satisfied with it."

Unlike Mantle, home runs were less important to him than base hits. Yet he is one of only three members of the 3,000 Hit Club who did not finish his career with a .300 lifetime average.

The numbers game was not always as important to the baseball player as it is today, though.

Take the case of Sam Rice, who played the outfield for the Washington Senators from 1915 to 1934. He ended up his career with a lifetime average of .322 and a total of 2,987 hits, just 13 short of the magic 3,000. But Rice, who had hit .293 and collected 98 hits in his final season, elected to retire. Had he been a modern-day performer, he undoubtedly would have played one more year in order to reach the prestigious milestone. Rice's decision to retire, though he didn't know it at the time, cost him baseball immortality. There are not too many modern-day fans who even recognize his name. A mere 13 additional hits would have added luster to his name. The present-day fans would then include him, in their minds, with the greatest hitters of all time.

"We didn't pay too much attention to records in those days," Rice said shortly before his death. "There wasn't so much emphasis put on them at the time. If I had it to do all over again, though, I think I would have hung around for a while. With all of this stress on records today, history has sort of cheated me, you know."

Sam Crawford was another player who looked back and rued the day that he retired. Today he is mostly remembered as an outfielder who played alongside Ty Cobb. But "Wahoo" Sam turned in a .309 lifetime average, led the major leagues in triples with 309, and proved to be the only player who has led both the National and American Leagues in home runs.

But he finished his career with 2,964 hits. He also could have played an extra year, as so many modern baseball players will do, and made the 3,000 Hit Club. Then perhaps he would have moved out of Cobb's shadow. But one hit shy of 3,000 is as distant as 1,000 short of the mark. Most baseball buffs know that Roberto Clemente ended up his career with 3,000 hits on the nose. But very few people realize that Rice and Crawford missed the mark by a whisker and could have hit it, if they had elected to do so.

Crawford legally deserves the 3,000 Hit Club recognition anyway. In 1899 he got 87 hits with Grand Rapids in the Western League. When the American League was formed in 1900, the National Commission ruled that any player from the Western League who entered either the National or American Leagues would be credited with all the hits that he had made in the Western League. But the statistician who compiled Crawford's lifetime average inadvertently overlooked those hits. So he finished his career with 2,964 hits instead of 3,051, to which he is entitled.

Crawford, it seems, was dealt a double twist of fate: he was victimized by the numbers game and the record book.

Lefty O'Doul was also cheated by the numbers game. The two-time batting champ in the National League finished his career with a .349 average. Yet he is not ranked with the top hitters of all time because the baseball rulesmakers say that he did not play the required ten years in order to qualify for such exalted distinction. Actually, O'Doul played 11 years in the big leagues. But the first four were spent as a pitcher. The record compilers don't count those years.

But the late irrepressible Irishman did. "I spent 11 years in the big leagues and ended up with a .349 average," he often said to the surprise of unknowing listeners. "That's lifetime average, not a single season's mark. Only Cobb, Hornsby, and Jackson ever did better. That's pretty good company."

O'Doul was also denied entrance into another elite club—the .400 Hitters—by a single base hit. In 1929 he batted .398, the closest that anyone has come to .400 without hitting it. (Harry Heilmann also hit .398. But, in another season, he batted .401.)

"Only eight hitters in the history of baseball ever hit .400," O'Doul said regretfully. "If an official scorer had ruled one of many plays a hit rather than an error, I would have been the ninth."

Babe Ruth didn't miss .400 by too much, either. In 1923 he hit .393 and didn't even win the batting title. (Heilmann did.) When people think of the Babe, they envision the legendary long-ball hitter. But they sometimes forget that he was a .342 lifetime hitter, too. If the Babe had been able to get three more hits in 1923, they would never be able to forget it.

Ten players in the history of the game have hit 50 or more runs in one season. You can probably name all of them. But can you recall the four players who did not hit 50, but did smack 49? Well, they are Lou Gehrig, Ted Kluszewski, Frank Robinson, and Harmon Killebrew.

"Close only counts in horseshoes," they say. So these four sluggers have been relegated to a lower echelon of long-ball hitters.

Billy Goodman wound up his major league career with a lifetime average of .300. Minnie Minoso hit .299. Is there a difference? Well, Minoso prevailed upon Chicago White Sox owner Bill Veeck to reactivate him, at the age of 57, in the final month of the 1976 season. You might say that Minoso thought there was a difference.

Pitchers have known their frustration in battling the numbers game, too. *The Baseball Encyclopedia* lists the leading winning percentage pitchers of all time from .600 up. Jack Chesbro and Ed Walsh, who won 41 and 40 games, respectively, in their best seasons (the highest numbers of wins by any pitchers in the history of the game), aren't listed, because they ended up their careers with the identical winning mark—.599!

Thirteen pitchers have won 30 or more games in one season. "Three-Finger" Brown, George Mullin, Ed Cicotte, and Hal Newhouser did not. They won 29. In the record book that looms as one very important win.

Spud Chandler, like Lefty O'Doul, has been footnoted out of the record book. The Yankees' right hander won 109 games and lost only 43 for a phenomenal winning percentage of .717. That's the best mark of all time for any pitcher who has won 100 or more games. But the rulesmakers say that a pitcher has to have recorded 200 victories in order to rank with the all-time best. So Whitey Ford (236–106) tops the list with a mark of .690.

Jim Bunning pitched no-hitters in both leagues. He won over 100 games in each league, too. And he also struck out more than 1,000 batters in each league. Overall, he struck out 2,855 batters. Another 145 would have guaranteed him a bust in Cooperstown. He'll probably never make it, though.

Tom Seaver struck out 200 or more batters in nine consecutive years. That's a record. But his personal high of 289 is still far from the top. Ten pitchers have gone over 300 strikeouts in a season.

Roy Face still thinks about the one decision in 19 which he dropped in 1959. Nineteen and oh? Wouldn't that be something!

Vic Willis of the old Boston Braves might have welcomed one more loss, though. In 1905 he dropped 29 decisions. No one else has ever done that. But 30 losses? That would really single him out!

Early Wynn and Robin Roberts typify the modern-day players' conflict with the numbers game.

Wynn won only one game in 1963. That was his last major league victory. It was also his 300th career win. He got it in relief. That's struggling. With satisfaction, though.

Roberts struggled, too. In vain, though. Eleven years after his last 20-game season, he called it quits, 14 victories short of the coveted 300 Win Club.

Why did those Hall of Famers put so much time and toil into so few victories at the tail end of their careers? They did so because, competitive as baseball players are prone to be, they played the game to the hilt: until their number(s) were up.

To them, it wasn't any trivial matter!

Speaking of trivia, though, I've got a question for you: who were those two players, in addition to Al Kaline, who collected more than 3,000 lifetime hits but failed to finish their careers with an average of .300?

Answer: Lou Brock (.293) and Carl Yastrzemski (.288)

Chapter Nine

NICKNAMES

46. MATCHING NAMES

Match the following players with their nicknames.

Tommy Henrich	Walter Johnson
Carl Hubbell	Dom DiMaggio
Frankie Frisch	Tris Speaker
Honus Wagner	Ted Williams
Luke Appling	Casey Stengel
Johnny Mize	Vernon Law
Bobby Thomson	Ty Cobb
Allie Reynolds	Babe Ruth
Joe DiMaggio	Lou Gehrig
Paul Waner	Mickey Mantle

1) "The Staten Island Scott" _____
2) "The Super Chief" _____
3) "The Splendid Splinter" _____
4) "The Big Cat" _____
5) "The Little Professor" _____
6) "The Old Professor" _____
7) "Old Reliable" _____
8) "The Deacon" _____
9) "The Yankee Clipper" _____
10) "The Georgia Peach" _____
11) "The Flying Dutchman" _____
12) "The Grey Eagle" _____
13) "The Sultan of Swat" _____
14) "The Big Train" _____
15) "The Iron Horse" _____

16) "The Meal Ticket" _____
17) "The Commerce Comet" _____
18) "Old Aches and Pains" _____
19) "Big Poison" _____
20) "The Fordham Flash" _____

47. FIRST NAMES

Substitute the players' first names for their nicknames.

Edwin	Elwin
George	Jerome
Harry	Charles
Edward	Joe
James	Johnny
Leon	Leroy
Fred	Enos
Larry	Robert
Paul	Lynwood
Bill	Charles Dillon

1) "Moose" Skowron   ————
2) "Daffy" Dean   ————
3) "Dizzy" Dean   ————
4) "Yogi" Berra   ————
5) "Preacher" Roe   ————
6) "Snuffy" Stirnweiss   ————
7) "Flash" Gordon   ————
8) "Pepper" Martin   ————
9) "Schoolboy" Rowe   ————
10) "Duke" Snider   ————
11) "Casey" Stengel   ————
12) "Dixie" Walker   ————
13) "Peanuts" Lowrey   ————
14) "Satchel" Paige   ————
15) "Country" Slaughter   ————
16) "Chuck" Dressen   ————
17) "Whitey" Ford   ————
18) "Goose" Goslin   ————
19) "Lefty" Grove   ————
20) "Dusty" Rhodes   ————

48. MIDDLE NAMES

Place the following nicknames between the players' first and last names.

"The Whip"   "The Kid"
"Poosh 'Em Up" "Birdie"
"Pee Wee"   "The Crow"
"Bobo"   "The Barber"
"Three Finger"   "Home Run"
"Puddin' Head"   "The Lip"
"The Dutch Master" "King Kong"
"The Man"   "Pie"
"The Hat"   "Twinkletoes"
"The Cat"   "Louisiana Lightning"

1) Harry _____ Walker
2) Stan _____ Musial
3) Harry _____ Brecheen
4) Johnny _____ Vander Meer
5) Sal _____ Maglie
6) Ron _____ Guidry
7) Leo _____ Durocher
8) Ewell _____ Blackwell
9) Charlie _____ Keller
10) Willie _____ Jones
11) Frank _____ Crosetti
12) Frank _____ Baker
13) Tony _____ Lazzeri
14) Billy _____ Martin
15) Harold _____ Traynor
16) Louis _____ Newsom
17) George _____ Tebbetts
18) George _____ Selkirk
19) Mordecai _____ Brown
20) Harold _____ Reese

49. LAST NAMES

Match the players' last names with their nicknames and
their first names.

Doby	Reiser
Keeler	Murphy
Jones	Hubbell
Feller	Crawford
Jackson	Dugan
Piniella	Cochrane
Houk	Grimm
Medwick	Bottomley
Wood	Turner
Greenberg	Newhouser

1) "Ducky" Joe _____
2) "Wahoo" Sam _____
3) "Shoeless" Joe _____
4) "Smokey" Joe _____
5) "Jumping" Joe _____
6) "Sweet" Lou _____
7) "Hammerin' " Hank _____
8) "Blackjack" Mickey _____
9) "Rapid" Robert _____
10) "Jolly Cholly" _____
11) "Pistol" Pete _____
12) "Sunny" Jim _____
13) "Larrupin' " Larry _____
14) "Prince" Hal _____
15) "Major" Ralph _____
16) "Wee" Willie _____
17) "Fireman" Johnny _____
18) "Milkman" Jim _____
19) "Sad" Sam _____
20) "King" Carl _____

50. MULTIPLE NAMES

Supply the whole name.

1) "Dr. Strangeglove" _____
2) "Daddy Wags" _____
3) "The Seh Heh Kid" _____
4) "Charlie Hustle" _____
5) "The Vacuum Cleaner" _____

Supply the first name.

1) "Hondo" Howard _____
2) "Stretch" McCovey _____
3) "Tug" McGraw _____
4) "Killer" Killebrew _____
5) "Hawk" Harrelson _____

Supply the nickname.

1) Walter Williams _____
2) Jim Hunter _____
3) John Powell _____
4) John Odom _____
5) Jim Grant _____

Supply the last name.

1) "Sudden" Sam _____
2) "Gettysburg" Eddie _____
3) "Shake and Bake" _____
4) "Stonewall" Travis _____
5) "Vinegar Bend" _____

Answers

46. Matching Names

1) Bobby Thomson
2) Allie Reynolds
3) Ted Williams
4) Johnny Mize
5) Dom DiMaggio
6) Casey Stengel
7) Tommy Henrich
8) Vernon Law
9) Joe DiMaggio
10) Ty Cobb
11) Honus Wagner
12) Tris Speaker
13) Babe Ruth
14) Walter Johnson
15) Lou Gehrig
16) Carl Hubbell
17) Mickey Mantle
18) Luke Appling
19) Paul Waner
20) Frankie Frisch

47. First Names

1) Bill
2) Paul
3) Jerome
4) Larry
5) Elwin
6) George
7) Joe
8) Johnny
9) Lynwood
10) Edwin
11) Charles Dillon
12) Fred
13) Harry
14) Leroy
15) Enos
16) Charles
17) Edward
18) Leon
19) Robert
20) James

48. Middle Names

1) "The Hat"
2) "The Man"
3) "The Cat"
4) "The Dutch Master"
5) "The Barber"
6) "Louisiana Lightning"
7) "The Lip"
8) "The Whip"
9) "King Kong"
10) "Puddin' Head"

11) "The Crow"
12) "Home Run"
13) "Poosh 'Em Up"
14) "The Kid"
15) "Pie"

16) "Bobo"
17) "Birdie"
18) "Twinkletoes"
19) "Three Finger"
20) "Pee Wee"

49. Last Names

1) Medwick
2) Crawford
3) Jackson
4) Wood
5) Dugan
6) Piniella
7) Greenberg
8) Cochrane
9) Feller
10) Grimm

11) Reiser
12) Bottomley
13) Doby
14) Newhouser
15) Houk
16) Keeler
17) Murphy
18) Turner
19) Jones
20) Hubbell

50. Multiple Names

1) Dick Stuart
2) Leon Wagner
3) Willie Mays
4) Pete Rose
5) Brooks Robinson

1) "No-Neck"
2) "Catfish"
3) "Boog"
4) "Blue Moon"
5) "Mudcat"

1) Frank
2) Willie
3) Frank
4) Harmon
5) Ken

1) McDowell
2) Plank
3) McBride
4) Jackson
5) Mizell

Who's on First

Babe Herman looked like a knightly champion when he stepped into the batter's box—he hit .393 in 1930 and he batted .324 lifetime—but when he played the outfield or ran the bases, he seemed to develop some chinks in his armor.

Fly balls, the stories go, used to either bounce off his head or carom off his shoulders with great regularity. Some baseball observers have said that his glove was a mere ornament on his hand.

His base running didn't help the Brooklyn franchise lose its nickname of "Bums," either. Take the case of the day in 1926, for example, when the Dodgers hosted the Braves. The bases were full of Dodgers when Herman, a rookie at the time, advanced mightily to the plate. Hank DeBerry led off third, Dazzy Vance danced off second, and Chick Fewster leaned off first.

Herman did not disappoint them. He rocketed a ball high off the right field wall. DeBerry scored easily. Vance could have, too, but he changed his mind after taking a wide turn around third. He retreated to third base where he met Fewster sliding into the "hot corner." In the meantime, Herman got a good start out of the box. He put his head down and raced around the bases with reckless abandon. Sliding into third, with what he thought was a sure triple, he was perplexed to bump into his two teammates. You might call the Dodgers' base running, in that instance, a "comedy of errors," or you might label Herman's aggressive dash an example of a "rookie's mistake."

But the third baseman was confused, too. He knew that two of the runners didn't belong there, but he didn't know which two runners were trespassing. So he did the obvious: he tagged all three of the runners. And the umpire called two of them out. But which two? Who, do you think, had the right to be there?

Answer: Dazzy Vance, since there was no force, had rightful possession of the bag. Chick Fewster and Babe Herman, who were the trespassers, were declared out. Since that day, whenever someone says, "The Dodgers have three men on base," a listener with a keen sense of wit will invariably say, "Which one?"

Chapter Ten

THE HALL OF FAME

51. CLUES TO COOPERSTOWN

Match the following 50 Hall of Famers with their descriptions below.

Jackie Robinson	Josh Gibson
Zach Wheat	Ed Barrow
Herb Pennock	Eppa Rixey
Carl Hubbell	Fred Clarke
John McGraw	Jesse Haines
Bob Lemon	Babe Ruth
Bill Dickey	Ross Youngs
Hank Greenberg	Johnny Evers
Dazzy Vance	Satchel Paige
Al Simmons	Chick Hafey
Bill Terry	Edd Roush
Mel Ott	Goose Goslin
Branch Rickey	Max Carey
Heinie Manush	Frankie Frisch
Frank Baker	Lefty Gomez
Jimmy Collins	Sam Rice
Dave Bancroft	George Sisler
Red Faber	Monte Irvin
Bob Feller	Pie Traynor
Harry Hooper	Ray Schalk
Cool Papa Bell	Lou Boudreau
Nap Lajoie	Rabbit Maranville
Joe Cronin	Charlie Gehringer
Lou Gehrig	George Kelly
Ted Lyons	Robin Roberts

1) _____ This celebrated National League screwball artist won 253 major league games (24 in succession), pitched a 1–0 18-inning win against the Cardinals in 1933 (it wrapped up the pennant), and gained baseball immortality in the 1934 All Star Game when he struck out Babe Ruth, Lou Gehrig, Jimmie Foxx, Al Simmons, and Joe Cronin in succession.

2) _____ This slugging American League first baseman scored more than 100 runs in 13 consecutive seasons, batted in more than 100 runs in 13 consecutive seasons, and played in every one of his team's games for 13 consecutive seasons while, at one time or another, leading the league in almost every conceivable batting title.

3) _____ The fourth best winning percentage (.671) pitcher of all time, he also won 12 league home run titles.

4) _____ Part of a double-play trio immortalized in a famous poem, he had the good judgment to retrieve Al Bridwell's apparent hit and touch second base to force Fred Merkle on a play that pushed the Giants into a one-game playoff that they lost to the Cubs in 1908.

5) _____ A six-time home run champion, he hit more National League round-trippers with one team than any other left-handed batter.

6) _____ This American League outfielder, who won two batting titles (1930–31) and hit .334 lifetime, batted better than .380 four times, and hit better than .300 for four American League teams.

7) _____ Though he never played in a world series, he twice hit over .400, sported a .340 lifetime average, hit safely a record 257 times in one season, earned the reputation of being the best defensive first baseman of his time, and produced two sons who played in the majors.

8) _____ The last National Leaguer to hit over .400, he has been the Giants' most successful manager since John McGraw: he led New York to three pennants and one world title.

9) _____ A four-time home run champion who lost four peak years to the military service, he was discharged in mid-season of 1945, just in time to lead his team to pennant and world series victories.

134

10) _____ Winner of 286 major league games, he claims that his most satisfying victory was his pennant-clinching decision against the Dodgers in 1950.

11) _____ One of the most exciting base runners of all time, he led the Dodgers to six pennants and one world series victory between 1947–56; however, his greatest contribution came in 1949 when he was named the MVP for leading the league in batting (.342) and stolen bases (37). In that same year he drove home 124 runs and he scored 122 runs.

12) _____ Though he never won a world series game, he did win 266 lifetime contests, hurled three no-hitters, and pitched 12 one-hitters in his 18-year major league career.

13) _____ In a 22-year career, divided between the Phillies and the Reds, he won 266 games, the most victories by a National League southpaw until Warren Spahn recorded 363 triumphs.

14) _____ A pennant-winning manager in his first year, he was sold two years later, by Clark Griffith (his father-in-law), to the Red Sox for $250,000.

15) _____ Untainted catcher for the infamous Black Sox of 1919, he led American League receivers in putouts for nine years; fielding, eight years; and he caught over 100 games a season for 11 consecutive years.

16) _____ One of the four men who have won four consecutive home run titles, he starred in the infield for the Athletics (1908–14) and the Yankees (1916–22).

17) _____ One of the best defensive catchers who ever played the game, one of the best average-hitting catchers who ever played the game (.313), one of the best home run–hitting catchers who ever played the game (202), he played on eight world's championship clubs.

18) _____ Shortstop for the "Miracle Braves," he played with five National League teams over a 23-year span, during which time he established the major league shortstop record for putouts (5,139); and placed second in assists (7,354) and total chances (13,124).

19) _____ A three-time 20-game winner, he set a National League record when he led the loop in strikeouts for seven consecutive years.

20) _____ In 21 years of pitching in the American League, his team finished in the first division only five times (its highest finish was third); however this durable right hander won 260 games, a club record.

21) _____ Possessor of a 29-game batting streak, he played 18 years in the Dodgers' outfield while posting a .317 career batting mark and winning the 1918 batting championship with a .335 batting average.

22) _____ This Pirate outfielder, who stole 738 lifetime bases, led the National League in thefts for ten years. In 1922 he stole successfully 51 out of 53 times.

23) _____ A great defensive outfielder with the Reds and Giants (1916–31), he was also an accomplished batter, hitting .323 lifetime and winning batting championships in 1917 and 1919.

24) _____ He played in more games, registered more at-bats, scored more runs, collected more hits, slashed more doubles, slammed more triples, ran more total bases, and batted in more runs than any other Senator player.

25) _____ Second on the Tigers to Ty Cobb in games played, at-bats, runs, hits, doubles, and total bases, he starred in the 1934–35 world series and won the batting championship in 1937.

26) _____ Though he led the league in only one offensive department (triples, 19, in 1923), he batted .320 lifetime and gained baseball's admiration as the greatest defensive third baseman in National League history.

27) _____ A 240-game winner for the Athletics, Red Sox, and Yankees, he excelled in world series play with a spotless 5–0 record. He also saved three games in series competition.

28) _____ A .316 lifetime hitter, and manager of "The Gashouse Gang" that won the pennant and series in 1934, he was traded to the Cardinals for Rogers Hornsby.

29) _____ Considered by many to be the greatest third baseman to ever play the game, he revolutionized the style of third base play while compiling a .294 lifetime average and managing the Red Sox to back-to-back pennants in 1903–04.

30) _____ The first successful "boy manager"—he won consecutive pennants from 1901–3 and in 1909—he played 15 years in the Pirates' outfield while recording a .312 lifetime average.

31) _____ A .334-hitting third baseman, he gained greater fame when he led his charges to ten pennants and three world series victories.

32) _____ Winner of batting championships in 1901, 1903, and 1904, he once hit .422 for the Athletics, the highest single-season batting average in American League history.

33) _____ This .322 lifetime hitter for the Giants batted .300 in nine of his ten years in the majors while leading New York to five pennants and two world titles. At the age of 30, he died of a kidney ailment.

34) _____ Winner of 254 games, he was one of the four White Sox pitchers who won 20 games in 1920. During 15 of his 20 seasons in the majors, his team finished in the second division. He was also the last of the legal spitball pitchers in the American League.

35) _____ He played on five pennant winners with the Senators and the Tigers while compiling a .316 lifetime average. In 1928 he won the batting title with a .379 mark. Eleven times he drove home 100 runs.

36) _____ Though he did not get to the majors until he was 30, this outfielder for the Giants won an RBI title and finished his career with a .293 mark. In the 1951 series he batted .458 and stole home once.

37) _____ First baseman for the Giants, Reds, and Dodgers (1915–32), he batted .297. He once hit three home runs in three consecutive innings. At another time he banged seven home runs in six games.

38) _____ The oldest rookie in the history of the game (42), he posted a 6–1 record in 1948 to help the Indians win the pennant. At the age of 59, he pitched his last game for the Athletics. Dizzy Dean called him the greatest pitcher he had ever seen.

39) _____ This American League left hander was 6–0 in world series play and 3–1 in all-star action. He was also a four-time 20-game winner with an overall record of 189–102.

40) _____ The last player-manager who led his team to a pennant and world series victory, he owns a .295 lifetime average. He had his greatest year in 1948 when he hit .355, got four hits in the playoff game, and won the most valuable player award.

41) _____ He recorded a .317 lifetime average despite poor eyesight. For six consecutive years he batted better than .329. In 1929 the flyhawk, who played with both the Cardinals and the Reds, hit safely ten consecutive times to tie a league record.

42) _____ They called him "Beauty," because, in his time, he was considered a shortstop without a peer. In 1922 he set a record when he handled 984 chances at shortstop for the Giants. He averaged 5.97 chances a game during his major league career.

43) _____ Considered the best defensive outfielder, next to Tris Speaker, during his time, he was responsible for talking Ed Barrow into converting Babe Ruth into an outfielder. Along with Speaker and Duffy Lewis, he played in one of the most famous outfields of all time. A great world series performer, he turned in his best season's batting marks in 1921 and 1924 with the White Sox.

44) _____ He didn't come up to the majors until he was 27, but he won 210 games before he pitched his last major league ball at the age of 44. In the 1926 world series he beat the Yankees twice.

45) _____ He was likened to Willie Keeler with the bat, Tris Speaker in the field, and Ty Cobb on the bases. Yet this all-round performer never got a chance to show his skills in the majors. He was limited to 29 summers of Negro ball and 21 winters of off-season play.

46) _____ He won four batting titles and hit almost 800 home runs in the Negro leagues. Twice he hit more than 70 home runs in a season. He died at the age of 35, the year Jackie Robinson was admitted to the major leagues.

47) _____ A player, manager, and general manager, "The Mahatma" reached greatness in the game as an innovative administrator. He established the first farm system with the Cardinals, he broke the color line when he

signed Jackie Robinson, and he created dynasties in St. Louis and Brooklyn.

48) _____ The manager of the 1918 Red Sox world championship team, he is more singularly remembered for having discovered Honus Wagner, converting Babe Ruth into an outfielder, and establishing a dynasty as general manager of the Yankees.

49) _____ Winner of two games in the 1948 world series and loser of two games in the 1954 world series, he started out as a third baseman and ended up winning 207 major league games.

50) _____ A .330 lifetime hitter, he won one batting title (Tigers), collected 200 hits four times, and batted .300 for four major league clubs.

51. Clues to Cooperstown

1) Carl Hubbell	26) Pie Traynor
2) Lou Gehrig	27) Herb Pennock
3) Babe Ruth	28) Frankie Frisch
4) Johnny Evers	29) Jimmy Collins
5) Mel Ott	30) Fred Clarke
6) Al Simmons	31) John McGraw
7) George Sisler	32) Nap Lajoie
8) Bill Terry	33) Ross Youngs
9) Hank Greenberg	34) Red Faber
10) Robin Roberts	35) Goose Goslin
11) Jackie Robinson	36) Monte Irvin
12) Bob Feller	37) George Kelly
13) Eppa Rixey	38) Satchel Paige
14) Joe Cronin	39) Lefty Gomez
15) Ray Schalk	40) Lou Boudreau
16) Frank Baker	41) Chick Hafey
17) Bill Dickey	42) Dave Bancroft
18) Rabbit Maranville	43) Harry Hooper
19) Dazzy Vance	44) Jesse Haines
20) Ted Lyons	45) Cool Papa Bell
21) Zach Wheat	46) Josh Gibson
22) Max Carey	47) Branch Rickey
23) Edd Roush	48) Ed Barrow
24) Sam Rice	49) Bob Lemon
25) Charlie Gehringer	50) Heinie Manush

Who's on First

The 1919–20 Chicago White Sox, referred to infamously in history books as the "Black Sox," had a staggering array of talent.

In the season before they were declared ineligible to play professional baseball—for allegedly conspiring to fix the 1919 world series—Joe Jackson batted .382, Happy Felsch hit .338, and Buck Weaver averaged .333. Moundsmen Claude "Lefty" Williams and Ed Cicotte won 22 and 21 games, respectively. Chick Gandil and Swede Risberg were solid starters, and Fred McMullin was a valuable utility man. It's little wonder that the White Sox, who were the best team in baseball at the time, did not win another pennant, after 1919, for another 40 years. Their roster was razed.

If it were not for the scandal, Jackson, Weaver, and Cicotte would be comfortably enshrined at the Baseball Hall of Fame in Cooperstown, N. Y. Felsch and Williams might be, too.

The notoriety of the trial of the disqualified players, however, detracted from the honorable records of the Sox stalwarts who transcended the alleged temptation and remained unsullied by the scandal.

History books have paid more attention to the barred players than they have to the untainted stars who managed to win their niche in Cooperstown. There were three such players. If you can name two of them, you deserve a special niche of your own.

Answer: Ray Schalk, catcher; Eddie Collins, second baseman; and Red Faber, pitcher

Chapter Eleven

THE YANKEE FAN

52. A PROUD PAST

The Yankees have been the most successful team in the history of baseball. They have won a total of 32 pennants and 22 world series. See if you can name some of the players who have figured so prominently in their rich tradition.

1) The Yankee pitcher who lost a no-hitter and the game on the last pitch of a world series contest.

2) The Yankee batter whom Al Gionfriddo robbed of a home run with a game-saving catch in the 1947 world series.

3) The Yankee batter whom Sandy Amoros denied of a game on the last pitch of a world series contest.
series.

4) The Yankee infielder whose only two hits in a series were homers.

5) The former Yankee infielder who played for the Cubs against his ex-mates in the 1932 get-together.

6) The Yankee pitcher who threw the first official pitch in "old" Yankee Stadium and the ceremony pitch in "new" Yankee Stadium.

7) The flashy Yankee second baseman who led the league in errors in four of his first six years in the majors.

8) The Yankee infielder whose two-run homer turned back a Dizzy Dean bid to win a world series game in 1938.

9) The Yankee infielder whose 12th hit of the 1953 world series scored Hank Bauer with the series-deciding run in the sixth game.

10) The one-time National League great who played on five consecutive world championship teams for the Yankees.

11) The Yankee infielder who batted 1.000 in the 1947 world series on three safe pinch-hits.

12) The Yankee pitcher who saved the final games of the 1951 and 1952 world series.

13) The Yankee infielder who played three different positions—one in each series—on three different world title teams.

14) The former Boston Brave pitching great who performed in three world series for the Yankees.

15) The former MVP with another team in the American League who pitched in two world series with the Yankees.

16) The Yankee outfielder who is famous for a 1939 world series collision at home plate with Ernie Lombardi.

17) The Yankee pitching great who hit 36 career home runs.

18) The Yankee infield great who was given his release on "Old Timers' Day" in 1956.

19) The Yankee outfielder who played a clutch role for the Bronx Bombers when Joe DiMaggio missed one half of the season in 1949 because of a heel injury.

20) The Yankee catcher who played left field against the Braves in the 1958 world series.

53. WORLD SERIES WINS

Can you name the Yankee opponents in the years in which they won the world's championship? Every initial franchise in the National League is involved.

1) _____ (1923)
2) _____ (1927)
3) _____ (1928)
4) _____ (1932)
5) _____ (1936)
6) _____ (1937)
7) _____ (1938)
8) _____ (1939)
9) _____ (1941)
10) _____ (1943)
11) _____ (1947)
12) _____ (1949)
13) _____ (1950)
14) _____ (1951)
15) _____ (1952)
16) _____ (1953)
17) _____ (1956)
18) _____ (1958)
19) _____ (1961)
20) _____ (1962)
21) _____ (1977)
22) _____ (1978)

54. WORLD SERIES DEFEATS

Can you name the Yankees' opponents in the years in which they lost the world series? Teams that are involved are the Dodgers, Reds, Cardinals, Pirates, Braves, and Giants.

1) _____ (1921)
2) _____ (1922)
3) _____ (1926)
4) _____ (1942)
5) _____ (1955)
6) _____ (1957)
7) _____ (1960)
8) _____ (1963)
9) _____ (1964)
10) _____ (1976)

55. MATCHING NUMBERS

Can you match the following players with their uniform numbers that are listed below: Gene Woodling, Mel Stottlemyre, Gil McDougald, Frank Crosetti, Joe Page, Don Larsen, Joe DiMaggio, Babe Ruth, Bob Turley, Lou Gehrig, Hank Bauer, Vic Raschi, Tommy Henrich, Clete Boyer, Mickey Mantle, Whitey Ford, Phil Rizzuto, Bobby Richardson, Yogi Berra, and Allie Reynolds.

1) _____ (1)
2) _____ (2)
3) _____ (3)
4) _____ (4)
5) _____ (5)
6) _____ (6)
7) _____ (7)
8) _____ (8)
9) _____ (9)
10) _____ (10)
11) _____ (11)
12) _____ (12)
13) _____ (14)
14) _____ (15)
15) _____ (16)
16) _____ (17)
17) _____ (18)
18) _____ (19)
19) _____ (22)
20) _____ (23)

56. THE (30) HOME RUN CLUB

Fifteen Yankees have hit 30 or more home runs in one season. Can you name them? Their season's high total, in addition to the year in which they attained it, is provided.

1) _____ (61) 1961
2) _____ (60) 1927
3) _____ (54) 1961
4) _____ (49) 1934
5) _____ (46) 1937
6) _____ (41) 1980
7) _____ (37) 1977
8) _____ (33) 1925
9) _____ (33) 1941
10) _____ (33) 1972
11) _____ (32) 1975
12) _____ (31) 1941
13) _____ (31) 1966
14) _____ (30) 1940
15) _____ (30) 1952 and 1956

57. STARTERS AND FINISHERS

The following players either began or concluded their careers with the Yankees. See if you can determine which way it was. Answer "S" for started and "C" for concluded.

1) Dixie Walker   _____
2) Leo Durocher   _____
3) Paul Waner   _____
4) Lew Burdette   _____
5) Johnny Allen   _____
6) Fred Merkle   _____
7) Jackie Jensen   _____
8) Hugh Casey   _____
9) Lefty O'Doul   _____
10) Johnny Mize   _____
11) Mark Koenig   _____
12) Johnny Murphy   _____
13) Tony Lazzeri   _____
14) Buddy Rosar   _____
15) Jim Turner   _____
16) Rocky Colavito   _____
17) Cliff Mapes   _____
18) Dale Long   _____
19) Earl Torgeson   _____
20) Ron Swoboda   _____

58. YANKEES FIRST AND LAST

Twenty of the players listed below spent their entire careers with the Yankees. Which ones?

Phil Rizzuto	Bobby Richardson
Bob Meusel	Joe Page
Lou Gehrig	Bill Dickey
Tony Lazzeri	Lefty Gomez
Red Rolfe	Spud Chandler
Joe Gordon	Bill Bevens
Jerry Coleman	Vic Raschi
Yogi Berra	Gil McDougald
Allie Reynolds	Gene Woodling
Whitey Ford	Eddie Lopat
Babe Ruth	Johnny Kucks
Tony Kubek	Andy Carey
Bill Skowron	Ellie Howard
Frank Crosetti	Mel Stottlemyre
Hank Bauer	Herb Pennock
Earle Combs	Waite Hoyt
Tommy Henrich	Thurman Munson
Charlie Keller	Graig Nettles
Joe Collins	Roy White
Bobby Brown	Ralph Houk

1) _____	11) _____
2) _____	12) _____
3) _____	13) _____
4) _____	14) _____
5) _____	15) _____
6) _____	16) _____
7) _____	17) _____
8) _____	18) _____
9) _____	19) _____
10) _____	20) _____

59. BREAKING IN

With what team did the one-time Yankees, who are listed in the left-hand column, begin their major league careers?

1) Babe Ruth   ———————
2) Johnny Mize   ———————
3) Bobby Shantz   ———————
4) Eddie Lopat   ———————
5) Gene Woodling   ———————
6) Roger Maris   ———————
7) Don Larsen   ———————
8) Red Ruffing   ———————
9) Johnny Sain   ———————
10) Enos Slaughter   ———————
11) Wes Ferrell   ———————
12) Jim Turner   ———————
13) Allie Reynolds   ———————
14) Bobo Newsom   ———————
15) Sal Maglie   ———————
16) George McQuinn   ———————
17) Jim Konstanty   ———————
18) Irv Noren   ———————
19) Virgil Trucks   ———————
20) Robin Roberts   ———————

60. BOWING OUT

With what teams did the former Yankees, listed in the left-hand column below, conclude their big league careers?

1) Roger Maris   _____
2) Babe Ruth   _____
3) Joe Gordon   _____
4) Joe Page   _____
5) Gene Woodling   _____
6) Hank Bauer   _____
7) Billy Johnson   _____
8) Tony Lazzeri   _____
9) Lefty Gomez   _____
10) George Stirnweiss   _____
11) Ernie Bonham   _____
12) Hank Borowy   _____
13) Johnny Lindell   _____
14) Frank Shea   _____
15) Billy Martin   _____
16) Bill Skowron   _____
17) Don Larsen   _____
18) Clete Boyer   _____
19) Johnny Allen   _____
20) Ralph Terry   _____

61. FROM START TO FINISH

Match the following players with their career batting averages: Bobby Richardson, Tommy Henrich, Enos Slaughter, Bill Dickey, Babe Ruth, Joe Gordon, Yogi Berra, Ben Chapman, Earle Combs, Johnny Mize, Mickey Mantle, Bill Skowron, Phil Rizzuto, Lou Gehrig, Bob Meusel, Tony Lazzeri, Ellie Howard, Red Rolfe, Frank Baker, and Joe DiMaggio.

1) _____ (.342)
2) _____ (.340)
3) _____ (.325)
4) _____ (.325)
5) _____ (.313)
6) _____ (.312)
7) _____ (.309)
8) _____ (.307)
9) _____ (.302)
10) _____ (.300)
11) _____ (.298)
12) _____ (.292)
13) _____ (.289)
14) _____ (.285)
15) _____ (.282)
16) _____ (.282)
17) _____ (.274)
18) _____ (.273)
19) _____ (.268)
20) _____ (.266)

52. A Proud Past

1) Bill Bevens
2) Joe DiMaggio
3) Yogi Berra
4) Aaron Ward (1922)
5) Mark Koenig
6) Bob Shawkey
7) Joe Gordon
8) Frank Crosetti
9) Billy Martin
10) Johnny Mize (1949–53)
11) Bobby Brown
12) Bob Kuzava
13) Gil McDougald
14) Johnny Sain
15) Bobby Shantz
16) Charlie Keller
17) Red Ruffing
18) Phil Rizzuto
19) Tommy Henrich
20) Elston Howard

53. World Series Wins

1) Giants
2) Pirates
3) Cardinals
4) Cubs
5) Giants
6) Giants
7) Cubs
8) Reds
9) Dodgers
10) Cardinals
11) Dodgers
12) Dodgers
13) Phillies
14) Giants
15) Dodgers
16) Dodgers
17) Dodgers
18) Braves
19) Reds
20) Giants
21) Dodgers
22) Dodgers

54. World Series Defeats

1) Giants
2) Giants
3) Cardinals
4) Cardinals
5) Dodgers
6) Braves

7) Pirates
8) Dodgers
9) Cardinals
10) Reds

55. Matching Numbers

1) Bobby Richardson
2) Frank Crosetti
3) Babe Ruth
4) Lou Gehrig
5) Joe DiMaggio
6) Clete Boyer
7) Mickey Mantle
8) Yogi Berra
9) Hank Bauer
10) Phil Rizzuto
11) Joe Page
12) Gil McDougald
13) Gene Woodling
14) Tommy Henrich
15) Whitey Ford
16) Vic Raschi
17) Don Larsen
18) Bob Turley
19) Allie Reynolds
20) Mel Stottlemyre

56. The (30) Home Run Club

1) Roger Maris
2) Babe Ruth
3) Mickey Mantle
4) Lou Gehrig
5) Joe DiMaggio
6) Reggie Jackson
7) Graig Nettles
8) Bob Meusel
9) Charlie Keller
10) Bobby Murcer
11) Bobby Bonds
12) Tommy Henrich
13) Joe Pepitone
14) Joe Gordon
15) Yogi Berra

57. Starters and Finishers

1) S
2) S
3) C
4) S
5) S
6) C
7) S
8) C
9) S
10) C
11) S
12) S
13) S
14) S
15) C
16) C
17) S
18) C
19) C
20) C

154

58. Yankees First and Last

1) Phil Rizzuto
2) Lou Gehrig
3) Red Rolfe
4) Jerry Coleman
5) Whitey Ford
6) Tony Kubek
7) Frank Crosetti
8) Earle Combs
9) Tommy Henrich
10) Joe Collins
11) Bobby Brown
12) Bobby Richardson
13) Bill Dickey
14) Spud Chandler
15) Bill Bevens
16) Gil McDougald
17) Mel Stottlemyre
18) Thurman Munson
19) Roy White
20) Ralph Houk

59. Breaking In

1) Boston Red Sox
2) St. Louis Cardinals
3) Philadelphia Athletics
4) Chicago White Sox
5) Cleveland Indians
6) Cleveland Indians
7) St. Louis Browns
8) Boston Red Sox
9) Boston Braves
10) St. Louis Cardinals
11) Cleveland Indians
12) Boston Braves
13) Cleveland Indians
14) Brooklyn Dodgers
15) New York Giants
16) St. Louis Browns
17) Cincinnati Reds
18) Washington Senators
19) Detroit Tigers
20) Philadelphia Phillies

60. Bowing Out

1) St. Louis Cardinals
2) Boston Braves
3) Cleveland Indians
4) Pittsburgh Pirates
5) New York Mets
6) Kansas City Athletics
7) St. Louis Cardinals
8) New York Giants
9) Washington Senators
10) Cleveland Indians
11) Pittsburgh Pirates
12) Detroit Tigers
13) Philadelphia Phillies
14) Washington Senators
15) Minnesota Twins
16) California Angels
17) Chicago Cubs
18) Atlanta Braves
19) New York Giants
20) New York Mets

61. From Start to Finish

1) Babe Ruth
2) Lou Gehrig
3) Joe DiMaggio or Earle Combs
4) Earle Combs or Joe DiMaggio
5) Bill Dickey
6) Johnny Mize
7) Bob Meusel
8) Frank Baker
9) Ben Chapman
10) Enos Slaughter
11) Mickey Mantle
12) Tony Lazzeri
13) Red Rolfe
14) Yogi Berra
15) Tommy Henrich or Bill Skowron
16) Bill Skowron or Tommy Henrich
17) Ellie Howard
18) Phil Rizzuto
19) Joe Gordon
20) Bobby Richardson

Who's on First

There is a touch of irony in respect to the manner in which Lou Gehrig broke into the Yankees' lineup and the way in which he departed from it.

When the 1925 season started, Gehrig was the back-up first baseman. The first-string first sacker was a veteran of 12 years, a two-time home run champion, and the American League's leader in triples (19) the previous year. About one-third of the way through the season, though, the first stringer got hit in the head with a pitch; and he suffered from headaches for the remainder of the season. One day he asked manager Joe McCarthy for a game's rest. Lou Gehrig substituted for him and the rest of the story is history: the "Iron Horse" remained in the lineup for a record, 2,130 consecutive games. But he died a short two years after he hung up his cleats.

The player whom he replaced lived for 40 years after he departed from the Yankee lineup. Can you name him?

Answer: Wally Pipp

Chapter Twelve

BREAKING THE BARRIERS

62. DID THEY OR DIDN'T THEY?

Mark "T" or "F" for "True" or "False" before each statement.

1) _____ Don Newcombe hit more home runs (7) in one season than any other pitcher in the history of the National League.

2) _____ Roy Campanella hit more home runs (242) than any other catcher in National League history.

3) _____ Elston Howard hit a home run in his first world series at-bat.

4) _____ Bob Gibson was the first black pitcher to win the Cy Young Award.

5) _____ Two black pitchers have won the Cy Young Award in the same season.

6) _____ Richie Allen has been the only black third baseman to be named Rookie of the Year.

7) _____ Willie Mays has been the only black player to twice hit more than 50 home runs in a season.

8) _____ Bob Gibson once played for the Harlem Globetrotters.

9) _____ Elston Howard was the last Yankee to win the MVP Award.

10) _____ Ralph Garr's nickname is "The Road Runner."

11) _____ Roy Campanella won a record-tying three MVP awards.

12) _____ Willie Mays was the first player to collect more than 3,000 hits and 500 home runs.

13) _____ Frank Robinson was a unanimous choice as the American League's MVP in 1966.

14) _____ Matty and Felipe Alou have been the only brothers to finish one-two in a batting race.

15) _____ Jackie Robinson was the only black player to appear in the 1947 world series.

16) _____ Bobby Bonds has four times hit more than 30 home runs and stolen more than 40 bases in a season.

17) _____ Reggie Jackson has hit .300 in a season.

18) _____ Don Newcombe was the first black pitcher to win a series game.

19) _____ Larry Doby was the first black player to win the American League's MVP Award.

20) _____ Jackie Robinson was the first black player to win the National League's MVP Award.

21) _____ Hank Aaron, Roberto Clemente, and Lou Brock won the MVP Award.

22) _____ Reggie Jackson, when he hit three home runs in the final game of the 1977 series, delivered the four-base blows against three different pitchers.

23) _____ Willie Mays never won an RBI crown.

24) _____ No black player has ever won the Triple Crown.

25) _____ Don Newcombe lost all four of his pitching decisions in series play.

26) _____ Roy Campanella was the first black to hit a home run in series play.

27) _____ Larry Doby was the first black to hit two home runs in the same series.

28) _____ Hank Aaron was the first black to hit three home runs in a series.

29) _____ Jim Rice hit more home runs in one season than any other Red Sox player.

30) _____ Al Downing was the first black to appear in a world series game for the Yankees.

31) _____ Willie Mays never batted .300 nor hit a home run in series play.

32) _____ J. R. Richard has been the only black to strike out more than 300 batters in a season.

33) _____ Bob Gibson won more consecutive world series games than any other pitcher.

34) _____ Al Downing was the first black pitcher to win a series game for an American League team.

35) _____ The Dodgers opened the 1966 world series against the Orioles with six black players in their starting lineup.

36) _____ Bob Gibson was the last pitcher to win three games in a series.

37) _____ Dave Cash has had more at-bats in one season than any other major leaguer.

38) _____ Ferguson Jenkins has won more games than any other black pitcher.

39) _____ Willie McCovey played in four decades of major league ball.

40) _____ Jackie Robinson recorded the highest lifetime average (.311) of any black or hispanic player who finished his career with at least ten years of active service.

41) _____ Curt Flood handled 538 consecutive chances without making an error.

42) _____ Maury Wills ranks number two to Lou Brock in the number of career steals by a National Leaguer.

43) _____ Willie Mays scored the run in the 1962 series which snapped Whitey Ford's scoreless inning skein at 33 and two-thirds innings.

44) _____ Zoilo Versalles, Rod Carew, and Reggie Jackson have won the MVP Award in the American League.

45) _____ Willie Mays has a higher lifetime batting average than Mickey Mantle.

46) _____ Before Bill Madlock won back-to-back batting titles (1975–76), the last black or hispanic player in the National League to perform the feat was Tommy Davis (1962–63).

47) _____ Jackie Robinson was the last player in the series to execute a steal of home that was not on the front end of a double theft.

48) _____ Dick Allen won home run titles in both leagues.

63. THE TRAILBLAZERS

The following black or hispanic players were the first ones to perform for teams that previously were exclusively white: Larry Doby, Hank Thompson-Willard Brown, Sam Hairston, Bob Trice, Carlos Paula, Valmy Thomas, Jackie Robinson, Curt Roberts, Elston Howard, Hank Thompson–Monte Irvin, Ozzie Virgil, Sam Jethroe, Pumpsie Green, Ernie Banks–Gene Baker, Joe Black, and Tom Alston–Brooks Lawrence. Match the players with their respective teams.

1) _____ Browns
2) _____ Pirates
3) _____ Phillies
4) _____ Yankees
5) _____ Athletics
6) _____ Indians
7) _____ Cubs
8) _____ Reds
9) _____ Red Sox
10) _____ Senators
11) _____ Dodgers
12) _____ Braves
13) _____ Cardinals
14) _____ Giants
15) _____ Tigers
16) _____ White Sox

64. BLACK CLOUTERS

Thirteen black players have won a total of 29 league home run titles. (Ties count as wins.) Match the following players with the number of times they have won the crown: George Foster, Jim Rice, Larry Doby, Hank Aaron, Dick Allen, Willie Mays, Frank Robinson, Reggie Jackson, Willie McCovey, Willie Stargell, Ernie Banks, George Scott, and Ben Oglivie.

1) _____ (4)
2) _____ (4)
3) _____ (3)
4) _____ (3)
5) _____ (2)
6) _____ (2)
7) _____ (2)
8) _____ (2)
9) _____ (2)
10) _____ (2)
11) _____ (1)
12) _____ (1)
13) _____ (1)

65. SINGLE-SEASON SLUGGERS

Fourteen black players hold the single-season high in home runs for their respective clubs. (Two of them are co-holders of one club's mark.) The numbers of home runs and the teams are provided. The players are not. Two of the players hold the top position for two different teams.

1) _____ (52) San Francisco Giants
2) _____ (52) Cincinnati Reds
3) _____ (51) New York Giants*
4) _____ (49) Baltimore Orioles
5) _____ (47) Oakland A's
6) _____ (47) Atlanta Braves**
7) _____ (38) San Diego Padres
8) _____ (37) Chicago White Sox
9) _____ (37) California Angels***
10) _____ (37) Houston Astros
11) _____ (34) Kansas City Royals
12) _____ (30) Toronto Blue Jays

* Johnny Mize is the co-holder of this record.
** Eddie Mathews of the 1953 Milwaukee Braves is the co-holder of this record.
*** Two black ballplayers share this mark.

66. NATIONAL LEAGUE BATTING CHAMPS

Eleven black or hispanic players have won the National League batting title a total of 18 times: Bill Madlock, Ralph Garr, Matty Alou, Roberto Clemente, Jackie Robinson, Billy Williams, Willie Mays, Rico Carty, Tommy Davis, Dave Parker, and Hank Aaron. Match the players with the years in which they copped the crown(s). One of them won the title four times. Four of them won it twice.

1) _____ (1949)
2) _____ (1954)
3) _____ (1956)
4) _____ (1959)
5) _____ (1961)
6) _____ (1962)
7) _____ (1963)
8) _____ (1964)
9) _____ (1965)
10) _____ (1966)
11) _____ (1967)
12) _____ (1970)
13) _____ (1972)
14) _____ (1974)
15) _____ (1975)
16) _____ (1976)
17) _____ (1977)
18) _____ (1978)

67. AMERICAN LEAGUE BATTING CHAMPS

Five black or hispanic players—Alex Johnson, Frank Robinson, Tony Oliva, Rod Carew, and Bobby Avila— have won the American League batting title a total of 13 times. Match the players with the years in which they copped the crown(s). One of them did it seven times, one of them did it three times, and three of them did it once.

1) _____ (1954)
2) _____ (1964)
3) _____ (1965)
4) _____ (1966)
5) _____ (1969)
6) _____ (1970)
7) _____ (1971)
8) _____ (1972)
9) _____ (1973)
10) _____ (1974)
11) _____ (1975)
12) _____ (1977)
13) _____ (1978)

68. ROOKIES OF THE YEAR

Six of the first seven Rookie of the Year awards in the National League went to black players: Sam Jethroe, Jim Gilliam, Don Newcombe, Willie Mays, Joe Black, and Jackie Robinson. Can you place them in their proper order?

1) _____ (1947)
2) _____ (1949)
3) _____ (1950)
4) _____ (1951)
5) _____ (1952)
6) _____ (1953)

69. THE HALL OF FAME

Fifteen black or hispanic players have been elected to the Hall of Fame. You should be able to name at least seven of them. If you can name ten, though, you're entitled to a little bit of fame for yourself.

1) _____
2) _____
3) _____
4) _____
5) _____
6) _____
7) _____
8) _____
9) _____
10) _____
11) _____
12) _____
13) _____
14) _____
15) _____

Answers

62. Did They or Didn't They?

1) False (Don Drysdale hit seven twice.)
2) False (Johnny Bench, (356)
3) True (1955)
4) False (Don Newcombe, 1956)
5) True (Ferguson Jenkins, Cubs, and Vida Blue, A's, in 1971)
6) True
7) True (51 in 1955 and 52 in 1965)
8) True
9) False (Thurman Munson, 1976)
10) True
11) True (1951, 1953, and 1955)
12) False (Hank Aaron)
13) True
14) True (1966)
15) False (Dan Bankhead did, too.)
16) True (1969, 1973, 1977–78)
17) True
18) False (Joe Black, 1952)
19) False (Elston Howard, 1963)
20) True (1949)
21) False (Lou Brock did not.)
22) True (Burt Hooton, Elias Sosa, and Charlie Hough)
23) True
24) False (Frank Robinson, 1966)
25) True
26) False (Larry Doby, 1948)
27) False (Jim Gilliam, 1953)
28) True (1957)
29) False
30) False (Marshall Bridges, 1962)
31) True
32) True (1978–79)
33) True (7)
34) False (Mudcat Grant, 1965)
35) True (Maury Wills, Jim Gilliam, John Roseboro, Tommy Davis, Willie Davis, and Lou Johnson)
36) False (Mickey Lolich, 1968)
37) False
38) True (259)
39) True (The 1950s, the 1960s, the 1970s, and the 1980s)
40) False (Roberto Clemente, .317)
41) True (1965–67)
42) False (Max Carey

had 738; Wills, 586.)
43) True
44) True
45) True (.302–.298)

46) False (Roberto Clemente, 1964–65)
47) True (1955)
48) False (He won two AL titles, 1972 and 1974.)

63. The TrailBlazers

1) Thompson-Brown
2) Roberts
3) Thomas
4) Howard
5) Trice
6) Doby
7) Banks-Baker
8) Black
9) Green
10) Paula
11) Robinson
12) Jethroe
13) Alston-Lawrence
14) Thompson-Irvin
15) Virgil
16) Hairston

64. Black Clouters

1) Willie Mays or Hank Aaron
2) Hank Aaron or Willie Mays
3) Willie McCovey or Reggie Jackson
4) Willie McCovey or Reggie Jackson
5–10) Any combination of Larry Doby, Dick Allen, Willie Stargell, Ernie Banks, Jim Rice, or George Foster
11) Frank Robinson or George Scott or Ben Oglivie
12) Frank Robinson or George Scott or Ben Oglivie
13) Frank Robinson or George Scott or Ben Oglivie

65. Single-Season Sluggers

1) Willie Mays
2) George Foster
3) Willie Mays
4) Frank Robinson
5) Reggie Jackson
6) Hank Aaron
7) Nate Colbert
8) Dick Allen
9) Leon Wagner and Bobby Bonds
10) Jimmy Wynn
11) John Mayberry
12) John Mayberry
13) Willie Horton

66. National League

1) Robinson	10) Alou
2) Mays	11) Clemente
3) Aaron	12) Carty
4) Aaron	13) Williams
5) Clemente	14) Garr
6) Davis	15) Madlock
7) Davis	16) Madlock
8) Clemente	17) Parker
9) Clemente	18) Parker

67. American League

1) Avila	8) Carew
2) Oliva	9) Carew
3) Oliva	10) Carew
4) Robinson	11) Carew
5) Carew	12) Carew
6) Johnson	13) Carew
7) Oliva	

68. Rookies of the Year

1) Robinson	4) Mays
2) Newcombe	5) Black
3) Jethroe	6) Gilliam

69. The Hall of Fame

1–15) Any combination of the following players:

Jackie Robinson	Roberto Clemente
Roy Campanella	Monte Irvin
Satchel Paige	Judy Johnson
Buck Leonard	Ernie Banks
Josh Gibson	John "Pop" Lloyd
Cool Papa Bell	Martin Dihigo
	Willie Mays
	Oscar Charleston
	Hank Aaron

Who's on First

Everything is not always black and white in baseball. But in the following two instances it was.

In the fourth game of the 1957 world series, with the Yankees leading the host Braves by the score of 5–4 in the tenth inning, a pinch-hitter came to the plate for Warren Spahn. A pitch from Tommy Byrne to the pinch-hitter was called a ball. But the substitute batter, who claimed that the ball had hit him, retrieved it and showed the enlightened Augie Donatelli a smudge of black shoe polish on the spheroid. Bob Grim relieved Byrne and was greeted with a game-tying double by Johnny Logan and a game-winning homer by Eddie Mathews. So the shoe polish call was a pivotal one.

In the fifth-and-final game of the 1969 world series, a similar-type play took place. In the sixth inning one of the host Mets was hit on the foot with a pitch by Dave McNally. Umpire Lou DiMuro called the pitch a ball. The batter protested. Upon inspection of the ball, DiMuro gave the hitter first base: he detected shoe polish on the ball. The shoe polish call once again proved to be pivotal. At the time the Mets were losing 3–0. But Donn Clendenon followed with a two-run homer, and the Mets were back in the game. Al Weis homered in the seventh to tie the game. The Mets went on to score the decisive two runs of a 5–3 series-clinching victory in the eighth on doubles by two Met outfielders and errors by two Oriole infielders.

Both of the players who figured prominently in the shoe polish plays had the same last name. That should give you a solid clue. Who are the two?

Answer: Nippy Jones and Cleon Jones

Chapter Thirteen

THE ALL-TIME TEAMS

70. THE ALL-TIME TEAMS

One of the three players listed below each position was chosen by the baseball fans—in 1969, baseball's centennial year—as the designated team's all-time best player at his respective position. Undoubtedly, if the poll were conducted today, many of the selectees would be replaced by players who have made their niche since that time. Looking back one decade, however, see how closely your selections match up with those that follow.

The Baltimore Orioles

1) First Base

a) Jim Gentile
b) Norm Siebern
c) Boog Powell

2) Second Base

a) Bob Johnson
b) Dave Johnson
c) Jerry Adair

3) Shortstop

a) Ron Hansen
b) Mark Belanger
c) Luis Aparicio

4) Third Base

a) Brooks Robinson
b) George Kell
c) Vern Stephens

5) Left Field

a) Don Buford
b) Gene Woodling
c) Al Smith

6) Center Field

a) Paul Blair
b) Curt Blefary
c) Jackie Brandt

7) Right Field

  a) Frank Robinson
  b) Russ Snyder
  c) Whitey Herzog

8) Catcher

  a) Ellie Hendricks
  b) John Orsino
  c) Gus Triandos

9) Pitcher
   (Right-hander)

  a) Wally Bunker
  b) Jim Palmer
  c) Milt Papas

10) Pitcher
    (Left-hander)

  a) Steve Barber
  b) Mike Cuellar
  c) Dave McNally

The Boston Red Sox

1) First Base

  a) Jimmie Foxx
  b) Rudy York
  c) Billy Goodman

2) Second Base

  a) Pete Runnels
  b) Bobby Doerr
  c) Billy Goodman

3) Shortstop

  a) Vern Stephens
  b) Rico Petrocelli
  c) Joe Cronin

4) Third Base

  a) George Kell
  b) Frank Malzone
  c) Lou Boudreau

5) Left Field

  a) Duffy Lewis
  b) Ted Williams
  c) Babe Ruth

6) Center Field

  a) Dom DiMaggio
  b) Jimmy Piersall
  c) Tris Speaker

7) Right Field

  a) Carl Yastrzemski
  b) Jackie Jensen
  c) Harry Hooper

8) Catcher

  a) Rick Ferrell
  b) Birdie Tebbetts
  c) Bill Carrigan

9) Pitcher
   (Right-hander)

   a) Joe Wood
   b) Ellis Kinder
   c) Cy Young

10) Pitcher
    (Left-hander)

   a) Babe Ruth
   b) Lefty Grove
   c) Mel Parnell

The Chicago White Sox

1) First Base

   a) Eddie Robinson
   b) Ted Kluszewski
   c) Zeke Bonura

2) Second Base

   a) Nellie Fox
   b) Don Kolloway
   c) Eddie Collins

3) Shortstop

   a) Luke Appling
   b) Luis Aparicio
   c) Chico Carrasquel

4) Third Base

   a) Jimmy Dykes
   b) Buck Weaver
   c) Willie Kamm

5) Left Field

   a) Minnie Minoso
   b) Al Simmons
   c) Gus Zernial

6) Center Field

   a) Joe Jackson
   b) Johnny Mostil
   c) Jim Landis

7) Right Field

   a) Taft Wright
   b) Harry Hooper
   c) Smead Jolley

8) Catcher

   a) Ray Schalk
   b) Sherman Lollar
   c) John Romano

9) Pitcher
   (Right-hander)

   a) Ed Walsh
   b) Ted Lyons
   c) Early Wynn

10) Pitcher
    (Left-hander)

   a) Claude Williams
   b) Gary Peters
   c) Billy Pierce

The Cleveland Indians

1) First Base
   a) Lew Fonseca
   b) Luke Easter
   c) Hal Trosky

2) Second Base
   a) Nap Lajoie
   b) Joe Gordon
   c) Bobby Avila

3) Shortstop
   a) Ray Chapman
   b) Joe Sewell
   c) Lou Boudreau

4) Third Base
   a) Al Rosen
   b) Ken Keltner
   c) Willie Kamm

5) Left Field
   a) Charlie Jamieson
   b) Joe Vosmik
   c) Dale Mitchell

6) Center Field
   a) Earl Averill
   b) Larry Doby
   c) Tris Speaker

7) Right Field
   a) Joe Jackson
   b) Rocky Colavito
   c) Elmer Smith

8) Catcher
   a) Jim Hegan
   b) Steve O'Neill
   c) Frank Hayes

9) Pitcher
   (Right-hander)

   a) Bob Feller
   b) Early Wynn
   c) Bob Lemon

10) Pitcher
    (Left-hander)

    a) Vean Gregg
    b) Gene Bearden
    c) Herb Score

The Detroit Tigers

1) First Base
   a) Lu Blue
   b) Norm Cash
   c) Hank Greenberg

2) Second Base
   a) Charlie Gehringer
   b) Dick McAuliffe
   c) Eddie Mayo

3) shortstop

   a) Harvey Kuenn
   b) Billy Rogell
   c) Donie Bush

4) Third Base

   a) George Kell
   b) Mike Higgins
   c) Marv Owen

5) Left Field

   a) Willie Horton
   b) Goose Goslin
   c) Harry Heilmann

6) Center Field

   a) Doc Cramer
   b) Ty Cobb
   c) Al Simmons

7) Right Field

   a) Sam Crawford
   b) Al Kaline
   c) Vic Wertz

8) Catcher

   a) Mickey Cochrane
   b) Birdie Tebbetts
   c) Bill Freehan

9) Pitcher
   (Right-hander)

   a) Frank Lary
   b) Jim Bunning
   c) Denny McLain

10) Pitcher
   (Left-hander)

   a) Mickey Lolich
   b) Hal Newhouser
   c) Billy Hoeft

The Minnesota Twins

1) First Base

   a) Vic Power
   b) Harmon Killebrew
   c) Don Mincher

2) Second Base

   a) Rod Carew
   b) Bernie Allen
   c) Billy Martin

3) shortstop

   a) Jackie Hernandez
   b) Frank Quilici
   c) Zoilo Versalles

4) Third Base

   a) Bill Tuttle
   b) Cesar Tovar
   c) Rich Rollins

5) Left Field

  a) Bob Allison
  b) Jim Lemon
  c) Sandy Valdespino

6) Center Field

  a) Lenny Green
  b) Ted Uhlaender
  c) Jimmie Hall

7) Right Field

  a) Joe Nossek
  b) Tony Oliva
  c) Bill Tuttle

8) Catcher

  a) Jerry Zimmerman
  b) Earl Battey
  c) John Roseboro

9) Pitcher
   (Right-hander)

  a) Camilo Pascual
  b) Jim Perry
  c) Dean Chance

10) Pitcher
    (Left-hander)

  a) Jim Merritt
  b) Jim Kaat
  c) Jack Kralick

The New York Yankees

1) First Base

  a) Bill Skowron
  b) Lou Gehrig
  c) Joe Pepitone

2) Second Base

  a) Joe Gordon
  b) Bobby Richardson
  c) Tony Lazzeri

3) shortstop

  a) Phil Rizzuto
  b) Frank Crosetti
  c) Tony Kubek

4) Third Base

  a) Clete Boyer
  b) Joe Dugan
  c) Red Rolfe

5) Left Field

  a) Mickey Mantle
  b) Charlie Keller
  c) Bob Meusel

6) Center Field

  a) Earle Combs
  b) Joe DiMaggio
  c) Mickey Mantle

7) Right Field

  a) Tommy Henrich
  b) Hank Bauer
  c) Babe Ruth

8) Catcher

  a) Bill Dickey
  b) Yogi Berra
  c) Elston Howard

9) Pitcher
   (Right-hander)

  a) Vic Raschi
  b) Allie Reynolds
  c) Red Ruffing

10) Pitcher
    (Left-hander)

  a) Whitey Ford
  b) Lefty Gomez
  c) Herb Pennock

The Washington Senators

1) First Base

  a) Mickey Vernon
  b) Joe Kuhel
  c) Joe Judge

2) Second Base

  a) Pete Runnels
  b) Buddy Myer
  c) Bucky Harris

3) Shortstop

  a) Joe Cronin
  b) Roger Peckinpaugh
  c) Cecil Travis

4) Third Base

  a) Eddie Yost
  b) Buddy Lewis
  c) Ossie Bluege

5) Left Field

  a) Goose Goslin
  b) Heinie Manush
  c) Frank Howard

6) Center Field

  a) Stan Spence
  b) Clyde Milan
  c) Sammy West

7) Right Field

  a) Buddy Lewis
  b) George Case
  c) Sam Rice

8) Catcher

  a) Muddy Ruel
  b) Rick Ferrell
  c) Jake Early

9) Pitcher
   (Right-hander)

   a) Early Wynn
   b) Walter Johnson
   c) Stan Coveleski

10) Pitcher
    (Left-hander)

    a) Tom Zachary
    b) Earl Whitehill
    c) George Mogridge

The Boston–Milwaukee–Atlanta Braves

1) First Base

   a) Joe Adcock
   b) Orlando Cepeda
   c) Earl Torgeson

2) Second Base

   a) Eddie Stanky
   b) Tony Cuccinello
   c) Red Schoendienst

3) Shortstop

   a) Al Dark
   b) Johnny Logan
   c) Rabbit Maranville

4) Third Base

   a) Bob Elliott
   b) Eddie Mathews
   c) Clete Boyer

5) Left Field

   a) Jeff Heath
   b) Hugh Duffy
   c) Sid Gordon

6) Center Field

   a) Felipe Alou
   b) Bill Bruton
   c) Wally Berger

7) Right Field

   a) Vince DiMaggio
   b) Tommy Holmes
   c) Henry Aaron

8) Catcher

   a) Del Crandall
   b) Ernie Lombardi
   c) Joe Torre

9) Pitcher
   (Choose two of five)

   a) Johnny Sain
   b) Lew Burdette
   c) Bob Buhl
   d) Charles "Kid"
      Nichols
   e) Warren Spahn

The Brooklyn–Los Angeles Dodgers

1) First Base

  a) Gil Hodges
  b) Dolph Camilli
  c) Jake Daubert

2) Second Base

  a) Tony Cuccinello
  b) Jackie Robinson
  c) Billy Herman

3) Shortstop

  a) Leo Durocher
  b) Maury Wills
  c) Pee Wee Reese

4) Third Base

  a) Billy Cox
  b) Cookie Lavagetto
  c) Jim Gilliam

5) Left Field

  a) Lefty O'Doul
  b) Zack Wheat
  c) Tommy Davis

6) Center Field

  a) Duke Snider
  b) Johnny Frederick
  c) Pete Reiser

7) Right Field

  a) Dixie Walker
  b) Carl Furillo
  c) Babe Herman

8) Catcher

  a) Al Lopez
  b) Roy Campanella
  c) John Roseboro

9) Pitcher
    (Right-hander)

  a) Dazzy Vance
  b) Don Newcombe
  c) Don Drysdale

10) Pitcher
    (Left-hander)

  a) Claude Osteen
  b) Sandy Koufax
  c) Preacher Roe

The Chicago Cubs

1) First Base

  a) Frank Chance
  b) Charlie Grimm
  c) Phil Cavarretta

2) Second Base

  a) Rogers Hornsby
  b) Johnny Evers
  c) Billy Herman

3) Shortstop

   a) Joe Tinker
   b) Billy Jurges
   c) Ernie Banks

4) Third Base

   a) Stan Hack
   b) Ron Santo
   c) Randy Jackson

5) Left Field

   a) Riggs Stephenson
   b) Hank Sauer
   c) Billy Williams

6) Center Field

   a) Hack Wilson
   b) Andy Pafko
   c) Augie Galan

7) Right Field

   a) Bill Nicholson
   b) Kiki Cuyler
   c) Harry Lowrey

8) Catcher

   a) Walker Cooper
   b) Gabby Hartnett
   c) Randy Hundley

9) Pitchers
   (Choose two of five)

   a) Mordecai Brown
   b) Charlie Root
   c) Ferguson Jenkins
   d) Ed Reulbach
   e) Larry French

The Cincinnati Reds

1) First Base

   a) Gordy Coleman
   b) Ted Kluszewski
   c) Frank McCormick

2) Second Base

   a) Don Blasingame
   b) Johnny Temple
   c) Hughie Critz

3) Shortstop

   a) Eddie Kasko
   b) Eddie Miller
   c) Roy McMillan

4) Third Base

   a) Grady Hatton
   b) Gene Freese
   c) Heinie Groh

5) Left Field

  a) Wally Post
  b) Pete Rose
  c) Rube Bressler

6) Center Field

  a) Vada Pinson
  b) Edd Roush
  c) Chick Hafey

7) Right Field

  a) Frank Robinson
  b) Sam Crawford
  c) Gus Bell

8) Catcher
  a) Ernie Lombardi
  b) Johnny Bench
  c) Ed Bailey

9) Pitcher
  (Right-hander)

  a) Paul Derringer
  b) Bucky Walters
  c) Ewell Blackwell

10) Pitcher
  (Left-hander)

  a) Joe Nuxhall
  b) Johnny Vander
     Meer
  c) Eppa Rixey

The New York–San Francisco Giants

1) First Base

  a) Willie McCovey
  b) Orlando Cepeda
  c) Bill Terry

2) Second Base

  a) Frankie Frisch
  b) Larry Doyle
  c) Eddie Stanky

3) Shortstop

  a) Al Dark
  b) Travis Jackson
  c) Dick Bartell

4) Third Base

  a) Heinie Groh
  b) Fred Lindstrom
  c) Hank Thompson

5) Left Field

a) Irish Meusel
b) Jo Jo Moore
c) Bobby Thomson

6) Center Field

a) Monte Irvin
b) Willie Mays
c) Don Mueller

7) Right Field

a) Mel Ott
b) Ross Youngs
c) Willard Marshall

8) Catcher

a) Walker Cooper
b) Wes Westrum
c) Harry Danning

9) Pitcher
(Right-hander:
Choose two of five)

a) Sal Maglie
b) Joe McGinnity
c) Juan Marichal
d) Jim Hearn
e) Christy Mathewson

10) Pitcher
(Left-hander:
Choose two of five)

a) Carl Hubbell
b) Rube Marquard
c) Johnny Antonelli
d) Dave Koslo
e) Art Nehf

The St. Louis Browns–Cardinals

1) First Base

a) Jim Bottomley
b) George Sisler
c) Bill White

2) Second Base

a) Red Schoendienst
b) Rogers Hornsby
c) Frankie Frisch

3) Shortstop

a) Dick Groat
b) Leo Durocher
c) Marty Marion

4) Third Base

a) Ken Boyer
b) Whitey Kurowski
c) Pepper Martin

5) Left Field

a) Joe Medwick
b) Lou Brock
c) Ken Williams

6) Center Field

a) Terry Moore
b) Curt Flood
c) Heinie Manush

7) Right Field

a) Billy Southworth
b) Enos Slaughter
c) Stan Musial

8) Catcher

a) Tim McCarver
b) Bob O'Farrell
c) Walker Cooper

9) Pitchers
(Choose two of five)

a) Bob Gibson
b) Dizzy Dean
c) Harry Brecheen
d) Mort Cooper
e) Urban Shocker

The Philadelphia Phillies

1) First Base

a) Ed Delahanty
b) Eddie Waitkus
c) Roy Sievers

2) Second Base

a) Cookie Rojas
b) Nap Lajoie
c) Emil Verban

3) Shortstop

a) Dick Groat
b) Dave Bancroft
c) Granny Hamner

4) Third Base

a) Willie Jones
b) Richie Allen
c) Pinky Whitney

5) Left Field

a) Lefty O'Doul
b) Dick Sisler
c) Del Ennis

6) Center Field

a) Harry Walker
b) Richie Ashburn
c) Gavvy Cravath

7) Right Field

a) Johnny Callison
b) Danny Litwhiler
c) Chuck Klein

8) Catcher

a) Jimmie Wilson
b) Smoky Burgess
c) Andy Seminick

9) Pitcher
(Right-hander)

a) Robin Roberts
b) Grover Alexander
c) Jim Bunning

10) Pitcher
(Left-hander)

a) Chris Short
b) Curt Simmons
c) Eppa Rixey

The Pittsburgh Pirates

1) First Base

a) Willie Stargell
b) Donn Clendenon
c) Gus Suhr

2) Second Base

a) Frankie Gustine
b) Danny Murtaugh
c) Bill Mazeroski

3) Short-stop

a) Honus Wagner
b) Dick Groat
c) Arky Vaughan

4) Third Base

a) Pie Traynor
b) Bob Elliott
c) Don Hoak

5) Left Field

a) Ralph Kiner
b) Paul Waner
c) Fred Clarke

6) Center Field

a) Matty Alou
b) Lloyd Waner
c) Bill Virdon

7) Right Field

a) Kiki Cuyler
b) Fred Linstrom
c) Roberto Clemente

8) Catcher

a) Walter Schmidt
b) Al Lopez
c) Smoky Burgess

9) Pitcher
   (Right-hander)

   a) Vernon Law
   b) Bob Friend
   c) Deacon Phillippe

10) Pitcher
    (Left-hander)

    a) Bob Veale
    b) Larry French
    c) Wilbur Cooper

Answers

70. The All-Time Teams

The Baltimore Orioles

- 1B) Boog Powell
- 2B) Jerry Adair
- SS) Luis Aparicio
- 3B) Brooks Robinson
- LF) Gene Woodling
- CF) Paul Blair
- RF) Frank Robinson
- C) Gus Triandos
- RH) Milt Pappas
- LH) Dave McNally

The Boston Red Sox

- 1B) Jimmie Foxx
- 2B) Bobby Doerr
- SS) Joe Cronin
- 3B) Frank Malzone
- LF) Ted Williams
- CF) Tris Speaker
- RF) Carl Yastrzemski
- C) Birdie Tebbetts
- RH) Cy Young
- LH) Lefty Grove

The Chicago White Sox

- 1B) Eddie Robinson
- 2B) Eddie Collins
- SS) Luke Appling
- 3B) Willie Kamm
- LF) Al Simmons
- CF) Johnny Mostil
- RF) Harry Hooper
- C) Ray Schalk
- RH) Ted Lyons
- LH) Billy Pierce

The Cleveland Indians

- 1B) Hal Trosky
- 2B) Nap Lajoie
- SS) Lou Boudreau
- 3B) Ken Keltner
- LF) Charlie Jamieson
- CF) Tris Speaker
- RF) Joe Jackson
- C) Steve O'Neill
- RH) Bob Feller
- LH) Vean Gregg

The Detroit Tigers

- 1B) Hank Greenberg
- 2B) Charlie Gehringer
- SS) Billy Rogell
- 3B) George Kell
- LF) Harry Heilmann
- CF) Ty Cobb
- RF) Al Kaline
- C) Mickey Cochrane
- RH) Denny McLain
- LH) Hal Newhouser

The Minnesota Twins

1B) Harmon Killebrew
2B) Rod Carew
SS) Zoilo Versalles
3B) Rich Rollins
LF) Bob Allison
CF) Ted Uhlaender
RF) Tony Oliva
C) Earl Battey
RH) Camilo Pascual
LH) Jim Kaat

The New York Yankees

1B) Lou Gehrig
2B) Tony Lazzeri
SS) Phil Rizzuto
3B) Red Rolfe
LF) Mickey Mantle
CF) Joe DiMaggio
RF) Babe Ruth
C) Bill Dickey
RH) Red Ruffing
LH) Whitey Ford

The Washington Senators

1B) Mickey Vernon
2B) Bucky Harris
SS) Joe Cronin
3B) Ossie Bluege
LF) Goose Goslin
CF) Clyde Milan
RF) Sam Rice
C) Muddy Ruel
RH) Walter Johnson
LH) Earl Whitehill

The Boston-Milwaukee-Atlanta Braves

1B) Joe Adcock
2B) Red Schoendienst
SS) Rabbit Maranville
3B) Eddie Mathews
LF) Hugh Duffy
CF) Felipe Alou
RF) Hank Aaron
C) Del Crandall
RH) Lew Burdette
LH) Warren Spahn

The Brooklyn–Los Angeles Dodgers

1B) Gil Hodges
2B) Jackie Robinson
SS) Pee Wee Reese
3B) Jim Gilliam
LF) Zach Wheat
CF) Duke Snider
RF) Dixie Walker
C) Roy Campanella
RH) Don Drysdale
LH) Sandy Koufax

The Chicago Cubs

1B) Charlie Grimm
2B) Rogers Hornsby
SS) Ernie Banks
3B) Ron Santo
LF) Billy Williams
CF) Hack Wilson
RF) Kiki Cuyler
C) Gabby Hartnett
RH) Charlie Root
LH) Larry French

1B) Ted Kluszewski
2B) Hughie Critz
SS) Roy McMillan
3B) Heinie Groh
LF) Pete Rose
CF) Edd Roush
RF) Frank Robinson
 C) Ernie Lombardi
RH) Bucky Walters
LH) Eppa Rixey

The New York–San Francisco Giants

1B) Bill Terry
2B) Frankie Frisch
SS) Al Dark
3B) Fred Lindstrom
LF) Bobby Thomson
CF) Willie Mays
RF) Mel Ott
 C) Wes Westrum
RH) Juan Marichal
RH) Christy Mathewson
LH) Carl Hubbell
LH) Johnny Antonelli

The St. Louis Browns–Cardinals

1B) George Sisler
2B) Rogers Hornsby

SS) Marty Marion
3B) Ken Boyer
LF) Joe Medwick
CF) Curt Flood
RF) Stan Musial
 C) Walker Cooper
RH) Bob Gibson
RH) Dizzy Dean

The Philadelphia Phillies

1B) Eddie Waitkus
2B) Cookie Rojas
SS) Granny Hamner
3B) Willie Jones
LF) Del Ennis
CF) Richie Ashburn
RF) Chuck Klein
 C) Andy Seminick
RH) Robin Roberts
LH) Chris Short

The Pittsburgh Pirates

1B) Gus Suhr
2B) Bill Mazeroski
SS) Honus Wagner
3B) Pie Traynor
LF) Paul Waner
CF) Lloyd Waner
RF) Roberto Clemente
 C) Walter Schmidt
RH) Deacon Phillippe
LH) Wilbur Cooper

Who's on First

The final game of the 1926 world series has gone down in baseball history as one of the most exciting finishes in the annals of the Fall Classic.

It certainly did not lack drama.

With the visiting Cardinals leading the Yankees 3–2 in the bottom of the sixth, Jesse Haines developed a finger blister while the Yankees loaded the bases with two out. Rogers Hornsby, the manager of St. Louis, decided to replace Haines with Grover Alexander, who had already won two games in the series. Alexander, one of the all-time greats of the hill, had to face Tony Lazzeri, a long-ball-hitting rookie. On the second pitch of the confrontation, Lazzeri almost decisively won the duel: he hit a long line drive to left that tailed a few feet left of the foul pole. Three pitches later, Alexander struck Lazzeri out on a sweeping curve ball.

In a groove, Alexander mowed the Yankees down in order in both the seventh and the eighth innings. He had retired nine consecutive batters before he faced Babe Ruth, with two outs, in the ninth. Working cautiously, he proceeded to walk the Babe. But Alex was still not out of danger. He had to face Bob Meusel, who had won the home run crown the year before. On the first pitch to Meusel, however, Ruth pulled the unexpected: he tried to steal second base. But the Cardinals' catcher threw a strike to Hornsby to nail Ruth, who became the first-and-only base runner to make the last out of a world series on an attempted steal.

After the series ended, owner Sam Breadon traded manager Hornsby to the Giants and named his catcher the team's manager. Maybe the backstop's final throw of the 1926 world series had something to do with the owner's decision.

Who was that veteran of 21 seasons who stopped the Yankees in 1926 and led the Cardinals in 1927?

Answer: Bob O'Farrell

189

Chapter Fourteen

THE HOT CORNER

71. WHAT'S THE RETIREMENT AGE?

Fifteen familiar names are listed with the dates on which they broke into the majors. You provide the dates, within two years, when they bowed out of the big leagues.

1) Luke Appling (1930–
2) Ernie Banks (1953–
3) Roy Campanella (1948–
4) Bob Feller (1936–
5) Harvey Haddix (1952–
6) Monte Irvin (1949–
7) Willie Jones (1947–
8) Ralph Kiner (1946–
9) Stan Musial (1941–
10) Mel Ott (1926–
11) Pee Wee Reese (1940–
12) Johnny Sain (1942–
13) Bobby Thomson (1946–
14) Mickey Vernon (1939–
15) Eddie Yost (1944–

72. ONE-TOWN MEN

Which ten of the following twenty players performed for the same club throughout their major league careers: Luke Appling, Brooks Robinson, Bill Terry, Stan Hack, Ralph Kiner, Lefty Grove, Joe Cronin, Walter Johnson, Grover Alexander, Mel Ott, Gil Hodges, Johnny Podres, Lew Burdette, Al Kaline, Ted Kluszewski, Ernie Banks, Cecil Travis, Pee Wee Reese, Eddie Mathews, and Dallas Green.

1) _____
2) _____
3) _____
4) _____
5) _____
6) _____
7) _____
8) _____
9) _____
10) _____

73. THE FIRST INNING

There have been 20 new major league franchises since 1953. Can you recall their first respective managers? The following list may give you a clue: Darrell Johnson, Ted Williams, Gene Mauch, Bob Kennedy, Harry Craft, Harry Lavagetto, Roy Hartsfield, Lou Boudreau, Charlie Grimm, Bill Rigney, Mickey Vernon, Casey Stengel, Joe Gordon, Preston Gomez, Dave Bristol, Joe Schultz, Bobby Bragan, Walt Alston, and Jimmy Dykes.

1) Milwaukee Braves (1953) _____
2) Baltimore Orioles (1954) _____
3) Kansas City A's (1955) _____
4) San Francisco Giants (1958) _____
5) Los Angeles Dodgers (1958) _____
6) Minnesota Twins (1961) _____
7) Washington Senators (1961) _____
8) Los Angeles Angels (1961) _____
9) Houston Astros (1962) _____
10) New York Mets (1962) _____
11) Atlanta Braves (1966) _____
12) Oakland A's (1968) _____
13) Kansas City Royals (1969) _____
14) Seattle Pilots (1969) _____
15) Montreal Expos (1969) _____
16) San Diego Padres (1969) _____
17) Milwaukee Brewers (1970) _____
18) Texas Rangers (1972) _____
19) Seattle Mariners (1977) _____
20) Toronto Blue Jays (1977 _____

74. THE LAST INNING

There have been ten major league franchises that have switched cities. Can you name the last respective managers of the original franchises? The following ten names should give you a start: Walt Alston, Harry Lavagetto, Charlie Grimm, Ted Williams, Joe Schultz, Marty Marion, Luke Appling, Eddie Joost, Bobby Bragan, and Bill Rigney.

1) Boston Braves _____ (1952)
2) St. Louis Browns _____ (1953)
3) Philadelphia A's _____ (1954)
4) New York Giants _____ (1957)
5) Brooklyn Dodgers _____ (1957)
6) Washington Senators _____ (1960)
7) Milwaukee Braves _____ (1965)
8) Kansas City A's _____ (1967)
9) Seattle Pilots _____ (1969)
10) Washington Senators _____ (1971)

75. SECONDARY PURSUITS

Match the following former players with the corresponding pursuits that they took up in their post-playing days.

1) _____ Vinegar Bend Mizell
2) _____ Joe Cronin
3) _____ Moe Berg
4) _____ Bobby Brown
5) _____ Billy Sunday
6) _____ George Moriarty
7) _____ Ralph Terry
8) _____ Johnny Berardino
9) _____ Al Schacht
10) _____ Red Rolfe
11) _____ Jim Brosnan
12) _____ Charlie Keller
13) _____ Greasy Neale
14) _____ Jim Thorpe
15) _____ Clark Griffith

a) Umpire
b) Actor
c) Congressman
d) Horse breeder
e) Secret agent
f) Pro football player
g) American League executive
h) Author
i) Pro football coach
j) Heart specialist
k) Golfer
l) Baseball club owner
m) Comedian ("Clown Prince of Baseball")
n) Athletic director of Dartmouth
o) Evangelist

76. MAJOR LEAGUE OWNERS

Some names of major league owners (past and present) are synonymous with the franchises they direct(ed). See how many of the following you can associate.

1) _____ Connie Mack
2) _____ Horace Stoneham
3) _____ Dan Topping
4) _____ Walter O'Malley
5) _____ Charles Comiskey
6) _____ Sam Breadon
7) _____ Tom Yawkey
8) _____ Lou Perini
9) _____ Bob Carpenter
10) _____ Bill Veeck
11) _____ Walter O. Briggs
12) _____ Clark Griffith
13) _____ Bob Short
14) _____ William Crosley
15) _____ Charles Finley
16) _____ Phillip K. Wrigley
17) _____ Mrs. Joan Payson
18) _____ Arthur Krock
19) _____ Calvin Griffith
20) _____ Gene Autry

a) The Reds
b) The Indians
c) The Dodgers
d) The Twins
e) The Athletics (Philadelphia)
f) The Tigers
g) The Cubs
h) The Giants
i) The Padres
j) The Yankees
k) The Braves
l) The Mets
m) The Rangers
n) The Phillies
o) The Cardinals
p) The White Sox
q) The Athletics (Oakland)
r) The Angels
s) The Senators
t) The Red Sox

77. THE MISSING LINK

Can you supply the third starting outfielder for the respective teams from the list of players that follow: Carl Furillo, Dick Sisler, Yogi Berra, Frank Robinson, Terry Moore, Roy White, Joe Rudi, Joe Gordon, Jackie Jensen, Al Simmons, Earle Combs, Vic Wertz, Don Mueller, Ted Williams, Jimmy Wynn, Reggie Smith, Roger Maris, Al Kaline, Charlie Keller, Cesar Cedeno, Harry Heilmann, Duffy Lewis, Casey Stengel, Matty Alou, and Pete Reiser.

1) Mickey Mantle, Roger Maris, and _____ (Yankees, 1961)

2) Joe DiMaggio, Tommy Henrich, and _____ (Yankees, 1941)

3) Stan Musial, Enos Slaughter, and _____ (Cardinals, 1942)

4) Tris Speaker, Harry Hooper, and _____ (Red Sox, 1916)

5) Babe Ruth, Bob Meusel, and _____ (Yankees, 1927)

6) Andy Pafko, Duke Snider, and _____ (Dodgers, 1952)

7) Dom DiMaggio, Al Zarilla, and _____ (Red Sox, 1950)

8) Bobby Bonds, Elliott Maddox, and _____ (Yankees, 1975)

9) Whitey Lockman, Willie Mays, and _____ (Giants, 1954)

10) Roberto Clemente, Willie Stargell, and _____ (Pirates, 1966)

11) Richie Ashburn, Del Ennis, and _____ (Phillies, 1950)

12) Lou Brock, Curt Flood, and _____ (Cardinals, 1968)

13) Ted Williams, Jimmy Piersall, and _____ (Red Sox, 1954)

14) Hoot Evers, Johnny Groth, and _____ (Tigers, 1950)

15) Willard Marshall, Bobby Thomson, and _____ (Giants, 1947)

16) Dixie Walker, Joe Medwick, and _____ (Dodgers, 1941)

17) Mule Haas, Bing Miller, and _____ (Athletics, 1931)

18) Ty Cobb, Heinie Manush, and _____ (Tigers, 1923)

19) Ross Youngs, Irish Meusel, and _____ (Giants, 1922)

20) Paul Blair, Don Buford, and _____ (Orioles, 1970)

21) Carl Yastrzemski, Tony Conigliaro, and _____ (Red Sox, 1970)

22) Willie Norton, Jim Northrup, and _____ (Tigers, 1969)

23) Jim North, Reggie Jackson, and _____ (Athletics, 1973)

24) Bob Watson, Jimmy Wynn, and _____ (Astros, 1973)

25) Bill Buckner, Willie Crawford, and _____ (Dodgers, 1974)

78. WHO PLAYED THIRD?

There have been many outstanding double-play combinations in the history of the major leagues. Twenty-five of the more recognizable ones, since 1940, are listed. Can you recall the third baseman who played in the same infield with them?

1) _____ Dave Johnson to Mark Belanger to Boog Powell (Orioles, '70)

2) _____ Dick Green to Bert Campaneris to Gene Tenace (A's, '74)

3) _____ Dave Cash to Larry Bowa to Willie Montanez (Phillies, '74)

4) _____ Dave Lopes to Bill Russell to Steve Garvey (Dodgers, '74)

5) _____ Joe Gordon to Phil Rizzuto to Johnny Sturm (Yankees, '41)

6) _____ Bobby Doerr to Joe Cronin to Jimmie Foxx (Red Sox, '41)

7) _____ Billy Herman to Pee Wee Reese to Dolph Camilli (Dodgers, '41)

8) _____ Red Schoendienst to Marty Marion to Stan Musial (Cardinals, '46)

9) _____ Joe Gordon to Lou Boudreau to Eddie Robinson (Indians, '48)

10) _____ Pete Suder to Eddie Joost to Ferris Fain (A's, '49)

11) _____ Bobby Doerr to Vern Stephens to Billy Goodman (Red Sox, '49)

12) _____ Jackie Robinson to Pee Wee Reese to Gil Hodges (Dodgers, '52)

13) _____ Mike Goliat to Granny Hamner to Eddie Waitkus (Phillies, '50)

14) _____ Ed Stanky to Al Dark to Whitey Lockman (Giants, '51)

15) _____ Billy Martin to Phil Rizzuto to Joe Collins (Yankees, '52)

16) _____ Bob Avila to Ray Boone to Luke Easter (Indians, '52)

17) _____ Johnny Temple to Roy McMillan to Ted Kluszewski (Reds, '54)

18) _____ Red Schoendienst to Johnny Logan to Joe Adcock (Braves, '58)

19) _____ Bill Mazeroski to Dick Groat to Dick Stuart (Pirates, '60)

20) _____ Bobby Richardson to Tony Kubek to Bill Skowron (Yankees, '61)

21) _____ Nellie Fox to Luis Aparicio to Roy Sievers (White Sox, '61)

22) _____ Julian Javier to Dick Groat to Bill White (Cardinals, '64)

23) _____ Gene Beckert to Don Kessinger to Ernie Banks (Cubs, '65)

24) _____ Lonny Frey to Billy Myers to Frank McCormick (Reds, '40)

25) _____ Cass Michaels to Pete Runnels to Mickey Vernon (Senators, '51)

79. BROTHER COMBINATIONS

Provide the first name of the other brother who played in the major leagues.

1) _____, Joe, Dom DiMaggio
2) _____, Rick Ferrell
3) _____, Walker Cooper
4) _____, Larry Sherry
5) _____, Jesse Barnes
6) _____, Jerome Dean
7) _____, Gaylord Perry
8) _____, Phil Niekro
9) _____, Stan Coveleski
10) _____, Henry Mathewson
11) _____, Matty, Felipe Alou
12) _____, Johnny O'Brien
13) _____, Joe Torre
14) _____, Tony Conigliaro
15) _____, Clete, Cloyd Boyer
16) _____, Bob Meusel
17) _____, George Dickey
18) _____, Henry Aaron
19) _____, Paul Waner
20) _____, Elliott Maddox
21) _____, Harry Walker
22) _____, Dick Sisler
23) _____, Marv Throneberry
24) _____, Tom, Tim, Joe, Frank Delahanty
25) _____, Hal Keller

80. NO HANDICAP

During the annals of major league baseball, there have been many players who had to overcome adversity in order to fulfill their lifelong ambitions. Five of them follow: Mordecai Brown, Pete Gray, Red Ruffing, John Hiller, and William Hoy. Match them with the physical impairments that they had.

1) _____ Missing toes
2) _____ Deaf and dumb
3) _____ Missing fingers
4) _____ Missing arm
5) _____ Heart condition

81. BASEBALL TRAGEDIES

Match the following players who died tragically—either during or shortly after their playing careers—with the year in which they passed away: Roberto Clemente, Kenny Hubbs, Harry Agganis, Lou Gehrig, Thurman Munson, Ray Chapman, and Ed Delahanty.

1) _____ (1903)
2) _____ (1920)
3) _____ (1941)
4) _____ (1955)
5) _____ (1964)
6) _____ (1972)
7) _____ (1979)

82. NO UNTOUCHABLES

It's pretty hard to conceive that the top three hitters who ever lived—Ty Cobb, Rogers Hornsby, and Joe Jackson—were traded from one team to another. That's been the case of many great players, though. Twenty-five players who ended up their careers with .300 or better lifetime averages are listed with the team with which they first made their name. Name the team to which they were either traded or sold.

1) _____ Ty Cobb (Tigers)
2) _____ Rogers Hornsby (Cardinals)
3) _____ Joe Jackson (Indians)
4) _____ Tris Speaker (Red Sox)
5) _____ Babe Ruth (Red Sox)
6) _____ George Sisler (Browns)
7) _____ Al Simmons (A's)
8) _____ Paul Waner (Pirates)
9) _____ Eddie Collins (A's)
10) _____ Jimmie Foxx (A's)
11) _____ Joe Medwick (Cardinals)
12) _____ Chuck Klein (Phillies)
13) _____ Frank Frisch (Giants)
14) _____ Hank Greenberg (Tigers)
15) _____ Johnny Mize (Cardinals)
16) _____ Mickey Cochrane (A's)
17) _____ Richie Ashburn (Phillies)
18) _____ George Kell (Tigers)
19) _____ Dixie Walker (Dodgers)
20) _____ Ernie Lombardi (Reds)
21) _____ Harvey Kuenn (Tigers)
22) _____ Hank Aaron (Braves)
23) _____ Willie Mays (Giants)
24) _____ Joe Cronin (Senators)
25) _____ Enos Slaughter (Cardinals)

83. WHEN DID THEY COME UP?

I.

See if you can match the players that follow with the year in which they first broke into the majors (if you are within one year of the actual season, before or after, count it as a correct answer): Tom Henrich, Warren Spahn, Red Schoendienst, Joe DiMaggio, Eddie Yost, George Kell, Joe Gordon, Stan Musial, Ted Williams, and Dom DiMaggio.

1) _____ (1936)   6) _____ (1941)
2) _____ (1937)   7) _____ (1942)
3) _____ (1938)   8) _____ (1943)
4) _____ (1939)   9) _____ (1944)
5) _____ (1940)   10) _____ (1945)

II.

We're in the post-war era now. See how you do with the following ten players (if you are within one year of the actual season, before or after, count it as a correct answer): Whitey Ford, Willie Mays, Yogi Berra, Rocky Colavito, Jackie Robinson, Hank Aaron, Al Kaline, Richie Ashburn, Jerry Coleman, and Eddie Mathews.

1) _____ (1946)   6) _____ (1951)
2) _____ (1947)   7) _____ (1952)
3) _____ (1948)   8) _____ (1953)
4) _____ (1949)   9) _____ (1954)
5) _____ (1950)   10) _____ (1955)

III.

We're moving into your wheelhouse now. Take a good cut at the following players (if you are within one year of the actual season, before or after, count it as a correct answer): Mel Stottlemyre, Roger Maris, Ed Kranepool, Frank Robinson, Maury Wills, Pete Rose, Catfish Hunter, Carl Yastrzemski, Juan Marichal, and Ron Fairly.

1) _____ (1956) 6) _____ (1961)
2) _____ (1957) 7) _____ (1962)
3) _____ (1958) 8) _____ (1963)
4) _____ (1959) 9) _____ (1964)
5) _____ (1960) 10) _____ (1965)

IV.

We're now in the present era. It's a home run contest. The pitches are coming right down the middle. See how you can do with the following offerings (if you are within one year of the actual season, before or after, count it as a correct answer): Fred Lynn, Cesar Cedeno, George Scott, Jim Rice, Rod Carew, Mike Schmidt, Dave Parker, Bobby Bonds, Chris Speier, and Thurman Munson.

1) _____ (1966) 6) _____ (1971)
2) _____ (1967) 7) _____ (1972)
3) _____ (1968) 8) _____ (1973)
4) _____ (1969) 9) _____ (1974)
5) _____ (1970) 10) _____ (1975)

Answers .

71. What's the Retirement Age?

1) 1950
2) 1971
3) 1957
4) 1956
5) 1965
6) 1956
7) 1961
8) 1955
9) 1963
10) 1947
11) 1958
12) 1955
13) 1960
14) 1960
15) 1962

72. One-Town Men

1) Luke Appling
2) Brooks Robinson
3) Bill Terry
4) Stan Hack
5) Walter Johnson
6) Mel Ott
7) Al Kaline
8) Ernie Banks
9) Cecil Travis
10) Pee Wee Reese

73. The First Inning

1) Charlie Grimm
2) Jimmy Dykes
3) Lou Boudreau
4) Bill Rigney
5) Walter Alston
6) Harry Lavagetto
7) Mickey Vernon
8) Bill Rigney
9) Harry Craft
10) Casey Stengel
11) Bobby Bragan
12) Bob Kennedy
13) Joe Gordon
14) Joe Schultz
15) Gene Mauch
16) Preston Gomez
17) Dave Bristol
18) Ted Williams
19) Darrell Johnson
20) Roy Hartsfield

74. The Last Inning

1) Charlie Grimm
2) Marty Marion
3) Eddie Joost
4) Bill Rigney
5) Walter Alston
6) Harry Lavagetto
7) Bobby Bragan
8) Luke Appling
9) Joe Schultz
10) Ted Williams

75. Secondary Pursuits

1) c
2) g
3) e
4) j
5) o
6) a
7) k
8) b
9) m
10) n
11) h
12) d
13) i
14) f
15) l

76. Major League Owners

1) e
2) h
3) j
4) c
5) p
6) o
7) t
8) k
9) n
10) b
11) f
12) s
13) m
14) a
15) q
16) g
17) l
18) i
19) d
20) r

77. The Missing Link

1) Yogi Berra
2) Charlie Keller
3) Terry Moore
4) Duffy Lewis
5) Earle Combs
6) Carl Furillo
7) Ted Williams
8) Lou Piniella

9) Don Mueller
10) Matty Alou
11) Dick Sisler
12) Roger Maris
13) Jackie Jensen
14) Vic Wertz
15) Sid Gordon
16) Pete Reiser
17) Al Simmons
18) Harry Heilmann
19) Casey Stengel
20) Frank Robinson
21) Reggie Smith
22) Al Kaline
23) Joe Rudi
24) Cesar Cedeno
25) Jimmy Wynn

78. Who Played Third?

1) Brooks Robinson
2) Sal Bando
3) Mike Schmidt
4) Ron Cey
5) Red Rolfe
6) Jim Tabor
7) Harry Lavagetto
8) Whitey Kurowski
9) Ken Keltner
10) Hank Majeski
11) Johnny Pesky
12) Billy Cox
13) Willie Jones
14) Hank Thompson
15) Gil McDougald
16) Al Rosen
17) Bobby Adams
18) Eddie Mathews
19) Don Hoak
20) Clete Boyer
21) Al Smith
22) Ken Boyer
23) Ron Santo
24) Billy Werber
25) Eddie Yost

79. Brother Combinations

1) Vince
2) Wes
3) Mort
4) Norm
5) Virgil
6) Paul
7) Jim
8) Joe
9) Harry
10) Christy
11) Jesus
12) Eddie
13) Frank
14) Billy
15) Ken
16) Emil
17) Bill
18) Tommie
19) Lloyd
20) Garry
21) Fred
22) Dave
23) Faye
24) Ed
25) Charlie

80. No Handicap

1) Red Ruffing
2) William "Dummy" Hoy
3) Mordecai "Three Finger" Brown
4) Pete Gray
5) John Hiller

81. Baseball Tragedies

1) Ed Delahanty
2) Ray Chapman
3) Lou Gehrig
4) Harry Agganis
5) Kenny Hubbs
6) Roberto Clemente
7) Thurman Munson

82. No Untouchables

1) Athletics
2) Giants
3) White Sox
4) Indians
5) Yankees
6) Senators
7) White Sox
8) Dodgers
9) White Sox
10) Red Sox
11) Dodgers
12) Cubs
13) Cardinals
14) Pirates
15) Giants
16) Tigers
17) Cubs
18) Red Sox
19) Pirates
20) Braves
21) Indians
22) Brewers
23) Mets
24) Red Sox
25) Yankees

83. When Did They Come Up?

I

1) Joe DiMaggio
2) Tommy Henrich
3) Joe Gordon
4) Ted Williams
5) Dom DiMaggio
6) Stan Musial

7) Warren Spahn
8) George Kell
9) Eddie Yost
10) Red Schoendienst

II

1) Yogi Berra
2) Jackie Robinson
3) Richie Ashburn
4) Jerry Coleman
5) Whitey Ford
6) Willie Mays
7) Eddie Mathews
8) Al Kaline
9) Hank Aaron
10) Rocky Colavito

III

1) Frank Robinson
2) Roger Maris

3) Ron Fairly
4) Maury Wills
5) Juan Marichal
6) Carl Yastrzemski
7) Ed Kranepool
8) Pete Rose
9) Mel Stottlemyre
10) Catfish Hunter

IV

1) George Scott
2) Rod Carew
3) Bobby Bonds
4) Thurman Munson
5) Cesar Cedeno
6) Chris Speier
7) Mike Schmidt
8) Dave Parker
9) Jim Rice
10) Fred Lynn

Who's on First

Ray Chapman, had he not been hit by an errant pitch by the Yankees' Carl Mays, might have ended up in the Hall of Fame.

A .278 lifetime hitter, the 29-year-old shortstop was just coming into his own right as a batsman, averaging over .300 in three of his last four years. And he was an accomplished base runner, stealing 233 career bases, including 52 in 1917, the most bases that any Indian had ever pilfered in one season until Miguel Dilone swiped 61 in 1980.

But the deuces were stacked against him on August 16, 1920. The number-two batter in the lineup that day, he stroked two hits—both of them doubles—scored two runs and stole two bases. Defensively, he made two assists, two putouts, and two errors. In fact, he was hit with two pitches by Mays. The second one killed him.

His replacement in the lineup, had Chapman not been killed by that ill-fated pitch, might not have ended up in the Hall of Fame. For he very well could have been relegated to years on the bench behind a blossoming star. But Chapman's back-up did go on to play 14 years in the big leagues. He averaged .312 lifetime and batted .300 ten times, including nine times in his first ten years in the majors. The one time that he failed to bat .300, he missed by just one point. But perhaps the most incredible story about this Hall of Famer was his ability to make contact. He averaged only eight strikeouts per season for 14 years. In his last nine seasons he whiffed just five times per year. And in both 1930 and 1932 he fanned only three times, the all-time low for a full-time player.

Who was this one-time Indian-Yankee star who got his best break on the day that Chapman got the worst break of any major league player?

Answer: Joe Sewell

210

Chapter Fifteen

TOUCHING ALL THE BASES

84. WHOM DID THEY PRECEDE?

See if you can determine whom the following players preceded at their positions in the field.

1) Bill White (Giants): a. Nippy Jones, b. Steve Bilko, c. Joe Torre, d. Orlando Cepeda

2) Tony Lazzeri (Yankees): a. George Stirnweiss, b. Frankie Crosetti, c. Joe Gordon, d. Jerry Priddy

3) Leo Durocher (Dodgers): a. Arky Vaughan, b. Pee Wee Reese, c. Billy Herman, d. Frenchy Bordagaray

4) Eddie Mathews (Braves): a. Clete Boyer, b. Dennis Menke, c. Frank Bolling, d. Roy McMillan

5) Bobby Thomson (Giants): a. Clint Hartung, b. Whitey Lockman, c. Willie Mays, d. Monte Irvin*

6) Harry Walker (Phillies): a. Richie Ashburn, b. Del Ennis, c. Dick Sisler, d. Bill Nicholson

7) Joe DiMaggio (Yankees): a. Cliff Mapes, b. Mickey Mantle, c. Johnny Lindell, d. Irv Noren

8) Dom DiMaggio (Red Sox): a. Jackie Jensen, b. Gene Stephens, c. Tommy Umphlett, d. Jimmy Piersall

9) Yogi Berra (Yankees): a. Elston Howard, b. John Blanchard, c. Jake Gibbs, d. Jesse Gonder

10) Del Crandall (Braves): a. Joe Torre, b. Del Rice, c. Stan Lopata, d. Bob Uecker

* Position: Center field.

85. WHOM DID THEY SUCCEED?

See if you can figure out whom the following players succeeded at their positions on the field.

1) Babe Dahlgren (Yankees): a. Nick Etten, b. George McQuinn, c. Wally Pipp, d. Lou Gehrig

2) Jackie Robinson (Dodgers): a. Eddie Miksis, b. Eddie Stanky, c. Cookie Lavagetto, d. Don Zimmer*

3) Chico Carrasquel (White Sox): a. Luke Appling, b. Cass Michaels, c. Don Kolloway, d. Willie Miranda

4) Brooks Robinson (Orioles): a. Vern Stephens, b. Billy Hunter, c. George Kell, d. Billy Goodman

5) George Selkirk (Yankees): a. Ben Chapman, b. Earle Combs, c. Bob Meusel, d. Babe Ruth

6) Carl Yastrzemski (Red Sox): a. Ted Williams, b. Clyde Vollmer, c. Sam Mele, d. Al Zarilla

7) Lou Brock (Cardinals): a. Enos Slaughter, b. Wally Moon, c. Stan Musial, d. Joe Cunningham

8) Roger Maris (Yankees): a. Tommy Henrich, b. Hank Bauer, c. Norm Siebern, d. Harry Simpson

9) John Roseboro (Dodgers): a. Roy Campanella, b. Bruce Edwards, c. Joe Pignatano, d. Rube Walker

10) Wes Westrum (Giants): a. Ernie Lombardi, b. Sal Yvars, c. Walker Cooper, d. Ray Mueller

* Position: Second base.

86. CHIPS OFF THE OLD BLOCK

The players who are listed below had fathers who preceded them to the major leagues. Name the source of the offspring.

1) _____ Dick Sisler
2) _____ Tom Tresh
3) _____ Mike Hegan
4) _____ Buddy Bell
5) _____ Doug Camilli
6) _____ Hal Lanier
7) _____ Bob Boone
8) _____ Bump Wills
9) _____ Roy Smalley
10) _____ Steve Trout

87. THE GAS HOUSE GANG

In the 1930s the St. Louis Cardinals had a colorful group of players who were known as the Gas House Gang. Match the Gas Housers with the nicknames that they acquired.

1) _____ James Collins   a) Ducky
2) _____ Frankie Frisch   b) Spud
3) _____ Leo Durocher   c) Wild
4) _____ Johnny Martin   d) Rip
5) _____ Joe Medwick   e) Dizzy
6) _____ Enos Slaughter   f) The Fordham Flash
7) _____ Virgil Davis   g) Daffy
8) _____ Jerome Dean   h) The Lip
9) _____ Paul Dean   i) Pepper
10) _____ Bill Hallahan   j) Country

88. THE YEAR OF ———

Fit the phrases listed below to the years to which they apply.

The Whiz Kids
The Amazin' Ones
The Hitless Wonders
Gionfriddo's Gem
Feller's Pick-off (?)
Sandy's Snatch
Maz's Sudden Shot
The Gas House Gang
Larsen's Perfect Game
The M&M Boys
Pesky's Pause
Home Run Baker
Murderers' Row

The Babe Calls His Shot
The Go-Go Sox
The Black Sox
The Wild Hoss of the Osage
Merkle's Boner
Mays's Miracle Catch
Ernie's Snooze
Billy the Kid
Alex's Biggest Strikeout
The Miracle Braves
Mickey's Passed Ball
The Miracle of Coogan's
   Bluff

1) ———— (1906)
2) ———— (1908)
3) ———— (1911)
4) ———— (1914)
5) ———— (1919)
6) ———— (1926)
7) ———— (1927)
8) ———— (1931)
9) ———— (1932)
10) ———— (1934)
11) ———— (1939)
12) ———— (1941)
13) ———— (1946)
14) ———— (1947)
15) ———— (1948)
16) ———— (1950)
17) ———— (1951)
18) ———— (1953)
19) ———— (1954)
20) ———— (1955)
21) ———— (1956)
22) ———— (1959)
23) ———— (1960)
24) ———— (1961)
25) ———— (1969)

89. THE MEN AT THE MIKE

Most teams have an announcer who becomes known in his bailiwick as the "voice" of the club. Some of the announcers who are listed in the left-hand column have called the play-by-play with more than one team. But they have made their reputations as "the voice" of one particular club. Match the "voice" with the respective team.

1) _____ Mel Allen
2) _____ Red Barber
3) _____ Russ Hodges
4) _____ Lindsey Nelson
5) _____ Curt Gowdy
6) _____ By Saam
7) _____ Bob Prince
8) _____ Vince Scully
9) _____ Waite Hoyt
10) _____ Chuck Thompson
11) _____ Dizzy Dean
12) _____ Jack Brickhouse
13) _____ Ernie Harwell
14) _____ Harry Carey
15) _____ Monte Clark

a) The Pirates
b) The Browns
c) The White Sox
d) The A's (Oakland)
e) The Reds
f) The Giants
g) The Yankees
h) The Tigers
i) The Dodgers (Brooklyn)
j) The Red Sox
k) The Cardinals
l) The Orioles
m) The Dodgers (Los Angeles)
n) The Mets
o) The Phillies

90. INFIELD INFLATION

The infield of the 1911 Philadelphia Athletics is said to have been worth $100,000; the infield of the 1948 A's is reported to have been valued at $1,000,000. Take the following ten players and place them at their respective positions: Stuffy McInnis, Hank Majeski, Frank Baker, Ferris Fain, Pete Suder, Jack Barry, Eddie Collins, Eddie Joost, Ira Thomas, and Buddy Rosar.

1911 Athletics
1B _____
2B _____
SS _____
3B _____
 C _____

1948 Athletics
1B _____
2B _____
SS _____
3B _____
 C _____

91. PEN NAMES

In the following pairs of names, see if you can distinguish the major league player from the major league writer. Which one was the artist on the diamond?

1) Grantland Rice—Del Rice
2) Dan Parker—Wes Parker
3) Fred Winchell—Walter Winchell
4) Woody Woodward—Stanley Woodward
5) Frank Sullivan—Ed Sullivan
6) Gary Schumacher—Hal Schumacher
7) Dick Williams—Joe Williams
8) Tom Meany—Pat Meany
9) Art Fowler—Gene Fowler
10) Frank Graham—Jack Graham
11) Quentin Reynolds—Carl Reynolds
12) Frank Adams—Babe Adams
13) Bill Dailey—Arthur Dailey
14) Don Gross—Milton Gross
15) Babe Young—Dick Young
16) Red Smith—Hal Smith
17) Babe Twombly—Wells Twombly
18) Earl Lawson—Roxie Lawson
19) Ray Murray—Jim Murray
20) Johnny Powers—Jimmy Powers

92. ALL-ROUND RECORDS

Match the players who are listed below with the modern marks that they set.

Dale Long   Don Hoak
Joe Nuxhall   Jack Chesbro
Christy Mathewson   Joe Adcock
Ty Cobb   Taylor Douthit
Hank Aaron   Chuck Klein
Babe Ruth   Willie McCovey
Johnny Mize   Joe Cronin
Jimmie Foxx

1) _____ He completed 48 games in one season.
2) _____ He hit three home runs in one game six times.
3) _____ He hit for 18 total bases in one game.
4) _____ He hit eight home runs in eight consecutive games.
5) _____ He struck out six times in one game.
6) _____ He batted .300 or better 23 years in succession.
7) _____ He won 20 or more games 12 years in succession.
8) _____ He slugged for an .847 average in one season.
9) _____ He pinch-hit home runs in both ends of a doubleheader.
10) _____ He was intentionally passed 45 times in one season.
11) _____ He walked six times in one game.
12) _____ He scored 100 or more runs 15 times.
13) _____ He recorded 547 outfield putouts in one season.
14) _____ He registered 44 outfield assists in one season.
15) _____ He pitched in the major leagues at the age of 15.

93. MAJOR LEAGUE RE

Match the players who are listed below v   the
records that they set.

Rudy York   Nellie Fox
Dave Philley   Ty Cobb
Tony Cloninger   Owen Wilson
Lou Brock   Tris Speaker
Lloyd Waner   Ralph Kiner
Lou Gehrig   Tony Oliva
Earl Webb   Willie Mays
Bob Nieman

1) _____ He was the only pitcher to hit two grand slams in the same game.
2) _____ He hit 23 lifetime grand slams.
3) _____ He pinch-hit safely nine consecutive times.
4) _____ He stole home 34 times in his career.
5) _____ He collected 793 lifetime doubles.
6) _____ He hit 67 doubles in one season.
7) _____ He hit 36 triples in one season.
8) _____ He hit 18 home runs in one month.
9) _____ He stole 118 bases in one season.
10) _____ He led the major leagues in home runs for six consecutive years.
11) _____ He sprayed 198 singles in one season.
12) _____ He hit four home runs in one game and three triples in another.
13) _____ He won league batting titles in his first two full seasons in the majors.
14) _____ He hit home runs in his first two big-league at-bats.
15) _____ He played 98 straight games without striking out.

94. MOUND SPECIALISTS

Match the pitchers who are listed below with the records that they set.

Ed Reulbach   Wes Ferrell
Mike Marshall   Jim Tobin
Ferdie Schupp   Early Wynn
Nolan Ryan   Jack Chesbro
Hoyt Wilhelm   John Hiller
Tom Seaver   Bob Feller
Ed Walsh   Dick Littlefield
Bruno Haas

1) _____ He won 41 games in one season.
2) _____ He posted an 0.90 ERA in one season.
3) _____ He recorded 38 saves in one season.
4) _____ He hit three home runs in one game.
5) _____ He walked 16 batters in a nine-inning game.
6) _____ He pitched for ten big league teams.
7) _____ He pitched shutouts in both ends of a doubleheader.
8) _____ He struck out 383 batters in one season.
9) _____ He walked 1,775 batters in his career.
10) _____ He walked 208 batters in one season.
11) _____ He pitched in 106 games in one season.
12) _____ He pitched 464 innings in one season.
13) _____ He appeared in 1,042 games.
14) _____ He hit 38 lifetime home runs.
15) _____ He struck out ten consecutive batters in one game.

95. League Records

Match the players who are listed below with the league records which they set. Eight of the records are National League marks.

Grover Alexander   Christy Mathewson
Hack Wilson   Joe McGinnity
Honus Wagner   Rogers Hornsby
Johnny Allen   Pete Rose
Bob Gibson   Hub Leonard

1) _____ He won 37 games in one season.
2) _____ He weaved a season's 1.01 ERA.
3) _____ He posted 88 lifetime shutouts.
4) _____ He hit 56 home runs in one season.
5) _____ He batted safely in 44 consecutive games.
6) _____ He posted a 1.12 ERA (in over 150 innings of pitching).
7) _____ He recorded a .938 (AL) season's pitching percentage.
8) _____ He batted .300 or better for 15 consecutive years.
9) _____ He pitched 434 innings in one season.
10) _____ He slugged for a .736 season's average.

96. UNIQUE OUTINGS

Fill in the blanks below from the following pitchers:
Jim Vaughn, Allie Reynolds, Bob Feller, Fred Toney,
Virgil Trucks, Leon Cadore, Leon Ames, Joe Oeschger,
Nolan Ryan, and Johnny Vander Meer.

1) _____ In the only double no-hit game for nine innings, which was decided by a tenth-inning infield single
by Jim Thorpe, who got the win and no-hitter?
2) _____ Who got the loss?
3) _____ Who struck out 21 batters in a 16-inning
game?
4) _____ Who threw an opening-day no-hitter for nine
innings but lost in the 13th, 3–0?
5) _____ Name the four pitchers who have thrown two
no-hitters in the same year.
6) _____ Who were the two pitchers who hooked up
in the 26-inning tie between the Dodgers and the
Braves?

97. ROOKIE RECORDS

Match the one-time rookie with the record he holds.

_____ 1) George Watkins	a)	145 RBI
_____ 2) Lloyd Waner	b)	223 hits
_____ 3) Wally Berger,	c)	367 total bases
Frank Robinson	d)	.373 batting
_____ 4) Joe DiMaggio		average
_____ 5) Ted Williams	e)	38 home runs

98. A STAR IS BORN

Match the players who are listed with the cities in which they were born.

1)	_____ Hank Aaron	a)	Omaha, Neb.
2)	_____ Johnny Bench	b)	Martinez, Calif.
3)	_____ Tommy Davis	c)	Hartford, N.C.
4)	_____ Al Kaline	d)	Mobile, Ala.
5)	_____ Brooks Robinson	e)	Beaumont, Tex.
6)	_____ Frank Robinson	f)	Oklahoma City,
7)	_____ Pete Rose		Oklahoma
8)	_____ Bob Gibson	g)	Little Rock, Ark.
9)	_____ Jim Hunter	h)	Cincinnati, Ohio
10)	_____ Frank McGraw	i)	Brooklyn, N.Y.
		j)	Baltimore, Md.

99. THE INTERNATIONAL PASTIME

Not all of the major leaguers in the history of baseball have been born on the mainland of the United States. Many of them have come from foreign states, countries, islands, territories, and provinces. See if you can match the players with their place of birth.

1) _____ Sandy Alomar
2) _____ Cesar Cedeno
3) _____ Bert Campaneris
4) _____ Rod Carew
5) _____ Dave Concepcion
6) _____ Irish McIlveen
7) _____ Jorge Orta
8) _____ Ferguson Jenkins
9) _____ Bobby Thomson
10) _____ Moe Drabowsky
11) _____ Elmer Valo
12) _____ Masanori Murakami
13) _____ Reno Bertoia
14) _____ Elrod Hendricks
15) _____ Andre Rodgers
16) _____ Mike Lum
17) _____ Al Campanis
18) _____ Jimmy Austin

a) Otsuki, Japan
b) Swansea, Wales
c) Gatun, Panama
d) Salinas, Puerto Rico
e) Chartham, (Ontario) Canada
f) Ozanna, Poland
g) Mantanzas, Cuba
h) Honolulu, Hawaii
i) Mazatian, Mexico
j) Santo Domingo, Dominican Republic
k) Nassau, Bahamas
l) Kos, Greece
m) Glasgow, Scotland
n) Ribnik, Czechoslovakia
o) St. Vito, Udine, Italy
p) Aragua, Venezuela
q) St. Thomas, Virgin Islands
r) Belfast, Ireland

Answers.

84. Whom Did They Precede?

1) Orlando Cepeda
2) Joe Gordon
3) Pee Wee Reese
4) Clete Boyer
5) Willie Mays

6) Richie Ashburn
7) Mickey Mantle
8) Jimmy Piersall
9) Elston Howard
10) Joe Torre

85. Whom Did They Succeed?

1) Lou Gehrig
2) Eddie Stanky
3) Luke Appling
4) George Kell
5) Babe Ruth

6) Ted Williams
7) Stan Musial
8) Hank Bauer
9) Roy Campanella
10) Walker Cooper

86. Chips off the Old Block

1) George Sisler
2) Mike Tresh
3) Jim Hegan
4) Gus Bell
5) Dolph Camilli

6) Max Lanier
7) Ray Boone
8) Maury Wills
9) Roy Smalley
10) Paul "Dizzy" Trout

87. The Gas House Gang

1) d
2) f
3) h
4) i
5) a

6) j
7) b
8) e
9) g
10) c

88. The Year of _____

1) The Hitless Wonders
2) Merkle's Boner
3) Home Run Baker
4) The Miracle Braves
5) The Black Sox
6) Alex's Biggest Strikeout
7) Murderers' Row
8) The Wild Hoss of the Osage
9) The Babe Calls His Shot
10) The Gas House Gang
11) Ernie's Snooze
12) Mickey's Passed Ball
13) Pesky's Pause
14) Gionfriddo's Gem
15) Feller's Pick-off (?)
16) The Whiz Kids
17) The Miracle of Coogan's Bluff
18) Billy the Kid
19) Mays' Miracle Catch
20) Sandy's Snatch
21) Larsen's Perfect Game
22) The Go-Go Sox
23) Maz's Sudden Shot
24) The M&M Boys
25) The Amazin' Ones

89. The Men at the Mike

1) g
2) i
3) f
4) n
5) j
6) o
7) a
8) m
9) e
10) l
11) b
12) c
13) h
14) k
15) d

90. Infield Inflation

1) Stuffy McInnis
2) Eddie Collins
3) Jack Barry
4) Frank Baker
5) Ira Thomas

1) Ferris Fain
2) Pete Suder
3) Eddie Joost
4) Hank Majeski
5) Buddy Rosar

91. Pen Names

1) Del Rice
2) Wes Parker
3) Fred Winchell
4) Woody Woodward
5) Frank Sullivan
6) Hal Schumacher
7) Dick Williams
8) Pat Meany
9) Art Fowler
10) Jack Graham
11) Carl Reynolds
12) Babe Adams
13) Bill Dailey
14) Don Gross
15) Babe Young
16) Hal Smith
17) Babe Twombly
18) Roxie Lawson
19) Ray Murray
20) Johnny Powers

92. All-Round Records

1) Jack Chesbro (1904)
2) Johnny Mize
3) Joe Adcock (1954)
4) Dale Long (1956)
5) Don Hoak
6) Ty Cobb
7) Christy Mathewson
8) Babe Ruth (1921)
9) Joe Cronin (1943)
10) Willie McCovey (1969)
11) Jimmie Foxx (1938)
12) Hank Aaron
13) Taylor Douthit
14) Chuck Klein
15) Joe Nuxhall (1944)

93. Major League Records

1) Tony Cloninger (1966)
2) Lou Gehrig
3) Dave Philley (1958–59)
4) Ty Cobb
5) Tris Speaker
6) Earl Webb (1931)
7) Owen Wilson (1912)
8) Rudy York (1937)
9) Lou Brock (1974)
10) Ralph Kiner (1947–52)
11) Lloyd Waner (1927)
12) Willie Mays
13) Tony Oliva (1964–65)
14) Bob Nieman (1951)
15) Nellie Fox (1958)

94. Mound Specialists

1) Jack Chesbro (1904)
2) Ferdie Schupp (1916)
3) John Hiller (1973)
4) Jim Tobin (1942)
5) Bruno Haas (1915)
6) Dick Littlefield
7) Ed Reulbach (1906)
8) Nolan Ryan (1973)
9) Early Wynn
10) Bob Feller (1938)
11) Mike Marshall (1974)
12) Ed Walsh (1908)
13) Hoyt Wilhelm
14) Wes Ferrell
15) Tom Seaver (1970)

95. League Records

1) Christy Mathewson
2) Hub Leonard
3) Grover Alexander
4) Hack Wilson
5) Pete Rose
6) Bob Gibson
7) Johnny Allen
8) Honus Wagner
9) Joe McGinnity
10) Rogers Hornsby

96. Unique Outings

1) Fred Toney
2) Jim Vaughn
3) Tom Cheney
4) Leon Ames
5) Johnny Vander Meer, Virgil Trucks, Allie Reynolds, and Nolan Ryan
6) Joe Oeschger and Leon Cadore

97. Rookie Records

1) d
2) b
3) e
4) c
5) a

98. A Star Is Born

1) d   6) e
2) f   7) h
3) i   8) a
4) j   9) c
5) g   10) b

99. The International Pastime

1) d   10) f
2) j   11) n
3) g   12) a
4) c   13) o
5) p   14) q
6) r   15) k
7) i   16) h
8) e   17) l
9) m   18) b

Who's on First

Sometimes we have a tendency to remember events which happened long ago better than those which occurred "only yesterday."

Take the case of Joe DiMaggio and Pete Rose, for example. Both of them manufactured big batting streaks, the longest in the history of their respective leagues. In 1941 DiMaggio hit safely in 56 consecutive games, which is the major league record; in 1978 Rose batted cleanly in 44 consecutive games, which is the modern-day National League record.

On the nights on which their respective streaks came to a close, they were handcuffed by a starting and a relieving pitcher. Much has been written about the duo of Indian pitchers who halted DiMaggio's streak. Jim Bagby, the son of a former 31-game season winner for the Indians, was the starter; Al Smith, who won 12 of 25 decisions that year, came on in relief.

So far little has been written about the two Brave pitchers who helped to stop Rose's streak. Undoubtedly, in time, they will become a more important trivia tandem. One of them was a rookie at the time; the other one was a journeyman relief pitcher.

I'll be surprised if you can name both of them. Can you?

Answer: Larry McWilliams (starter) and Gene Garber (reliever)

About the Author

Dom Forker was born the day Joe DiMaggio hit three for six in the fifth game of DiMaggio's first World Series. A coach and former college pitcher, the author teaches English and journalism in Frenchtown, New Jersey, where he lives with his wife and three sons. He is the author of ALMOST EVERYTHING YOU'VE EVER WANTED TO KNOW ABOUT BASEBALL and is currently at work on a World Series quiz book.

Ⓢ

More Sports Books from SIGNET

☐ **SEMI-TOUGH by Dan Jenkins.** "The funniest, raunchiest book ever written about football and football players."— *Playboy* A rip-roaring movie starring Burt Reynolds, Kris Kristofferson, and Jill Clayburgh. With 8 pages of movie photos. (#J8184—$1.95)

☐ **NORTH DALLAS FORTY by Peter Gent.** The sensational million-copy bestseller! Eight days in the life of a pro football player. Eight days that take you into the heart of a man, a team, a sport, a game, and the raw power and violence that is America itself. "A remarkable novel . . . devastating impact . . ."—*The New York Times* (#E8906—$2.50)

☐ **THE GAME OF THEIR LIVES by Dave Klein.** They were the heroes of the greatest pro football game ever played—the famous 1958 sudden-death championship. Now they relive that—and the long years since . . . "Human drama!"— Howard Cosell (#J7532—$1.95)

☐ **THE FIRST OFFICIAL NFL TRIVIA BOOK by Ted Brock and Jim Campbell.** Try naming the original teams of the American Football League of the 1960s. Who was professional football's first left-handed quarterback? Settle arguments, start arguments, and amaze guests with the words and numbers of the most minuscule significance imaginable! (#J9541—$1.95)

☐ **THE PRO FOOTBALL MYSTIQUE by Dave Klein.** Everything that the coaches, the players, and the media think they know about pro football and never wanted the fans to find out. The book that brings the game back to earth—and gives it back to the fans. (#J8353—$1.95)*

*Price slightly higher in Canada
